The Modern State of Israel and Biblical Prophecy

S. K. Haddad

III Clink Street

London | New York

Published by Clink Street Publishing 2015

Copyright © 2015

First edition.

ISBN: 978-1-910782-20-0
E-Book: 978-1-910782-21-7

To my dear brother Amin

Table of Contents

Introduction

I have never liked long introductions and therefore shall not do so. Suffice it to say that the book deals with subjects true to its title. It gives a brief history of the Jews at the beginning, then deals with the promised land, its peoples and its conquest. There are things in the Bible which are used by men to further their own theories whether they be true or not. For this reason I deal with certain verses from Daniel 9 and Revelation 20. It is stated by many that these verses are essential to the future of Israel and the coming of the Lord.

The biblical texts are quoted from the Authorized Version of the Bible, also known as the King James version.

Chapter One
A Short History of the
Jewish Dispersion

When the Lord Jesus Christ went about doing good, the Jews of his day wanted to make him king. He preached to them the kingdom of heaven, but they did not understand. They thought that he would deliver them from Roman bondage (Jn.6:15). It was in this vein that they cried: "Blessed be the kingdom of our father David, that cometh in the name of the Lord" (Mk.11:10). When they were disappointed in him they accused him before Pilate of claiming a worldly kingship like other kings of the earth (Lk.23:2; Jn.19:12). Even just before his ascension, the disciples showed their worldly thinking by asking: "Lord, wilt thou at this time restore again the kingdom to Israel?" (Acts 1:6). The restoration of the kingdom has been the hope of the Jewish people since the Assyrian and Babylonian captivities and is the desire of Christians today who interpret the prophetic scriptures in a literal manner.

It is easy to understand the aspiration of the Jews for a national home in Palestine when their history is considered. They have been forced from one country to another for many centuries at the whim of their overlords. It is right to give a brief account of their dispersion, with particular reference to the persecution and abuse which they suffered in their long history after the Babylonian exile.

The permanent scattering of the Jews began during the Assyrian and Babylonian exiles in the land known today as Iraq. The northern kingdom of Israel, whose capital was Samaria, fell to Assyria in 722 B.C. Many Jews fled to Egypt. The southern kingdom of Judah, whose capital was Jerusalem, survived until 586 B.C. when it fell to the Neo-Babylonians, the Chaldeans. The Temple was destroyed and many of the people, particularly the nobles, were carried into Babylon. The Chaldean or Babylonian empire had succeeded the Assyrian in Mesopotamia (Iraq) and Syria and Palestine and was itself conquered by the Medes and Persians. Cyrus II, the Great, a Persian, overthrew the supremacy of the Median kings, conquered Babylon and took possession of its territories. He issued the decree in 536, under the hand of God, for the return of the Judean exiles to Jerusalem. They returned in waves, but not all returned. A community remained in Iraq until recent times when the majority emigrated to Israel. The Babylonian community was replenished by refugees after the final defeat of the Maccabees and at the time of the final destruction of the Temple and during the Bar Kokhba revolt of 133–135 A.D. Following this revolt Hadrian renamed the ancient land of Israel and Judea, Aelia Palestina, hence the name of Palestine.

The second Temple was built around 515 B.C. Judea remained a Persian province until the defeat of the Persians by Alexander the Great in 333. After Alexander's death in Babylon in 323 his domain was divided among his generals. The Ptolemies ruled over Egypt and the Seleucids ruled over Syria. Palestine fell to the Ptolemies until 198 B.C. when it was snatched out of their hands by the Seleucid Antiochus III. Antiochus IV, called "Epiphanes", meaning 'visible god' or 'god manifest', converted the Temple into a shrine to Zeus in 167 B.C. Mattathias the priest, father of five sons who later became known as the Maccabees, was ordered to sacrifice a pig in his town near Jerusalem. A bloody conflict arose and the Maccabean revolt began. It is a story of heroism and endurance. The Maccabees established the Hasmonean dynasty in Judea which lasted until 63 B.C. when Judea became a vassal state of Rome. The Temple, which was enlarged by Herod the Great, was finally destroyed in 70 A.D.

During the third century B.C. Jews were to be found in North Africa, Asia Minor and the shores of the Black Sea in what is now Turkey, in Greece, eastern Europe, Syria, Lebanon and Palestine. They were in Rome, Spain, and Gaul (today's France and western Germany) by the first century. They entered as soldiers in the armies of their conquerors, as fugitives, or as slaves taken in war and as sellers of sundry goods in the trail of conquering armies. We read in Acts 2:9–11 of the Jews gathered in Jerusalem for the day of Pentecost. They were "Parthians, and Medes, and Elamites, and the dwellers of Mesopotamia, and in Judea, and Cappadocia, in Pontus, and Asia, Phrygia, and Pamphylia, in Egypt, and in the parts of Libya about Cyrene, and strangers of Rome, Jews and proselytes, Cretes and Arabians." This means they came from Persia and what are now Iraq, Turkey, Greece, Europe, North Africa and Arabia.

The first rabbinical academy was set up in Judea by Johanan ben Zakkai in the first century A.D. He aimed to preserve Jewish culture in the face of the destruction that was raging in Jerusalem in 70 A.D. The synagogue replaced the Temple in some respects. During the reign of

Hadrian, in 133 A.D., Simon bar Kosiba, also known as Bar Kokhba, claimed to be the messiah and rebelled against the Romans. The revolt failed, Bar Kokhba was killed in 135 and Judaism outlawed. The effect of the revolt was to diminish the number of Jews living in Palestine through slaughter and flight. Many fled to the Parthian province of Babylonia (Iraq) and probably to Arabia. Galilee replaced Judea as the seat of Jewish culture. Further Jewish scattering occurred during the middle of the third century when the Roman empire passed through hard economic times. Jewish life in Palestine declined gradually so that by the fifth century the Palestinian community was a minority of world Jewry.

As the Palestinian community declined, the Babylonian community flourished as did its rabbinical academies. An exilarchate was established there during Parthian rule and continued under Persian rule. The exilarch, a descendent of the house of David, was head of the Jewish people with powers to collect taxes from them and appoint judges over them to deal with Jewish matters according to Jewish law. Babylonia became the centre of Jewish culture when Palestine lost that role. The Babylonian Talmud was completed in contrast to the Palestinian Talmud. Despite this, there were periods of persecution in Babylonia between 226 A.D. and 260 and between 455 and 475, instigated by the Zoroastrian priesthood.

Christianity, which was legalised by Constantine I, the Great, in 311 A.D., was made the official religion of the Roman empire by Theodosius I toward the end of the fourth century. Constantine built an eastern capital at the site of the Greek town of Byzantion (Byzantium) in 330 and called it Constantinople (Istanbul today). The Roman empire became permanently divided in 395 into a western empire, whose capital was Rome, and an eastern empire, whose capital was Constantinople.

Rome was sacked by Visigothic (west Goths) Germanic tribes in 410 and by the Vandals in 455. The Visigoths ruled over Spain, the Ostrogoths (east Goths) over Italy, the Vandals over North Africa and the Franks over France and western Germany. The Vandals and Gothic tribes adopted Arian Christianity, which denied the eternity and deity of Christ. The Franks adopted Roman Catholic Christianity, while Constantinople and the Byzantine empire adopted Greek Orthodox Christianity. The Jews remained unmolested by the Arian tribes until 589 when the Visigothic king of Spain converted to Catholicism and ordered the conversion of the Jews or their expulsion. Most fled to France and North Africa, only to be expelled from central France in 629 and to take refuge eastward in the Rhineland and in southern France.

Constantinople outlasted Rome as a capital of an empire by almost one thousand years until it fell to the Muslim Ottoman Turks in 1453. The lot of the Jews in the Byzantine empire varied according to the whim of the emperor and influence of the clergy. Synagogues were destroyed or confiscated at the end of the fifth and the early part of the sixth centuries and further Jewish persecution took place in the eighth and ninth centuries so that many fled to the Crimea and the Balkans and southeastern Europe. They moved eventually from there across Russia. Outside the Byzantine empire, the Khazars, a tribe of partly Mongolian origin who lived between the Caspian and Black seas, converted to Judaism during the eighth century and augmented Russian and east European Jewry.

The king of the Himyar tribe in the Yemen converted to Judaism with his people early in the fifth century. Most of the Yemenite Jews who immigrated to Israel during the twentieth century stem from this origin. The king of the Himyars was defeated at that time by an Abyssinian (Ethiopian) Christian army that crossed the water for that purpose. Jews fled to other parts of Arabia until those in the east found themselves under new masters in the seventh century, namely the Arabs.

The Jewish confrontation with Muhammad was tragic. Two tribes were expelled from Madinah and the men of a third tribe massacred. The reason for the massacre was said to be that the tribe broke a covenant of peace with Muhammad. Most Arabian Jews went to Iraq.

Syria, Palestine and Egypt were part of the Byzantine empire and Iraq part of the Persian empire. These countries, together with Persia, were conquered by the Arabs by the year 641, twenty years after Muhammad's death. The Persian conquest took longer to consolidate. North Africa was conquered in 647 and Spain in 711. There followed five centuries of Jewish prosperity and an increase in Jewish learning, especially in Spain. The exilarchate, which had lapsed in Persia during the persecutions of the fifth century, was restored by the Arabs. It lasted until the early part of the thirteenth century. Most of the Old Testament was translated into Arabic by Saadia ben Joseph al-Fayyumi (882–942), who was born in Egypt and became head of the rabbinical academy in Sura, Iraq. His disagreements with the exilarch led to the weakening of the power of that institution. A rabbinical academy remained in Tiberias. There the Masoretic scholars punctuated the Hebrew text of the Bible and worked until the tenth century. They followed the example of the Arabs in placing signs by the letters of the alphabet to indicate their pronunciation. They also worked to fix the rules of Hebrew grammar, but the major part of this work was done in the academies of Iraq and by the Jews of Islamic Spain. The Jews and Christians in Islamic lands were denied certain civil liberties, but were allowed religious freedom. Jews moved from Iraq, Syria and Palestine to Egypt, North Africa and Spain.

The Jews fared better under Islam than in Christian Europe. The years of Jewish history and culture in Spain between 900 and 1200 are often referred to as the "golden age". The Jews were merchants, bankers, scientists, astronomers, poets, philosophers, physicians – at times to the Caliph's court – and government administrators. They contributed to the translation of Greek learning into Arabic and Latin. Jewish philosophers wrote many important works in Arabic. Despite this, there was a period of persecution under Islam in Egypt early in the eleventh century and in Spain about the middle of the twelfth century by Muslim Berbers from North Africa who came to the aid of the Muslim armies which were beleaguered by the Christian kings of Spain. Money lending was a particular field in which the Jews offered a service. Usury was forbidden by Islam and Christianity at that time. It was not legalised in England until 1571. Money lending gave the Jews power with European kings and nobles and with the common people. They could supply money for ransom or for raising an army. But this worked often to their disadvantage because of envy.

Spain had come under the control of Christian kings, except for Granada, by the year 1212. A severe persecution with massacres of Jews occurred in 1391 in Castile and Aragon instigated by monks. Many Jews converted to Christianity to escape death. The Spanish Inquisition was set up in 1480. It sought out converts to Christianity who remained Jews secretly. Muslim Granada fell to Ferdinand and Isabella in 1492. The Jews were expelled from Spain within months. They scattered across North Africa and

Egypt, to regions in Italy and Greece and to Palestine. Those in Portugal had to convert to Christianity in 1497 or leave the country.

The Jews of central Europe, France and England suffered other shares of disasters. When the first Crusade was called to free the holy places in Palestine from Muslim hands, the mob which formed in Europe was unruly and went about killing Jews and robbing their property at the instigation of priests and monks. Persecution thus fell into the hands of the common people and did not belong to the sovereign only. Thousands of Jews lost their lives at the hands of the Crusaders in central Europe in 1096. When Jerusalem fell to the Crusaders in 1099, the Jews fled for refuge into their synagogue, only to be burnt alive with their building. Muslims were massacred in the streets. By contrast, when Salah u-Ddeen (Saladin) recaptured Jerusalem in 1187, he exercised mercy toward all and no massacre of any kind took place.

The Jews entered England in 1066. Horrid accusations of the murder of Christian children, for the ritual use of their blood, first appeared in Norwich in 1144 and led to fierce persecution. Such blood libels spread into Europe, beginning in France in 1171 and then in Germany and other European states and persisted until the fifteenth century. Philip Augustus expelled the Jews from his domain around Paris in 1182, only to recall them for their financial services sixteen years later. Campaigns against usury took place in France during the next century with the clearing of debts owing to Jewish bankers. Accusations of blood libel and desecration of the host were made between 1288 and 1290. Expulsion from European cities was widespread in the fifteenth century: from Cologne in 1424, from Augsburg in 1439, from other regions of Germany between 1450 and 1500 and from Geneva in

1491. Persecution in Austria in 1421 followed accusations that the Jews assisted John Huss against the Roman Catholic Church.

Riots against Jews occurred in England at the start of the third Crusade. Massacres took place in various cities, particularly in York in 1190. One hundred years later the Jews were expelled from England by Edward I after a charge of counterfeiting money was raised against a few. Most went to France, only to be expelled from there in 1306. They were allowed again in France in 1315, then banished in 1359, then recalled in 1361, then expelled in 1394. They were permitted to return to England by Cromwell and began to settle in 1656.

The Plague, or Black Death, struck Europe in 1348. The Jews were accused of causing this disaster, through which hundreds of thousands died, by poisoning the water wells. Great massacres were carried out in central Europe and in France. Those who survived were expelled from the towns and settled in countries farther east.

Most Jews lived in Europe between the eleventh and fifteenth centuries. Although they settled in Russia and eastern Europe before the first crusade, the centuries of persecution which followed in central, western and southern Europe saw them taking refuge in the east in larger numbers. The Slavs, who were pushed eastward by German settlers, brigands and barons in the twelfth century, invited the Jews into Poland in 1264 and granted them protection under a charter. This was ratified and extended in 1344, 1364 and 1367. The Lithuanians welcomed them too. They entered Poland also from the Crimea, North Africa, the Byzantine empire and Spain and by the mid-seventeenth century were the largest European Jewish community. They were the Ashkenazim, largely of west German Jewry, but the term included the

Jews of northern France. The Spanish Jews were the Sephardim or eastern Jews.

An almost twenty year period of slaughter of Jews and Roman Catholics took place in the Polish Ukraine between 1648 and 1667 by the Greek Orthodox Cossacks of the Ukraine. The Poles, who were the landowners, had oppressed the Ukrainian peasants. The Jews were the land administrators. The Cossacks allied themselves with the Tartars for their acts of revenge. Poland was occupied between 1655 and 1667 by the Russians, who invaded from the northeast, and the Swedes, who invaded from the west. The Ukraine was later divided between Russia and Poland. Many Jews escaped to Germany and Holland. Those who remained had to suffer blood libels in the eighteenth century and massacres by Cossacks in the Polish Ukraine city of Uman in 1768.

The Jews in the east came under new but benevolent masters again. This time it was the Muslim Ottoman Turks who established an empire. Greece and the Balkans were conquered before Constantinople fell in 1453. During the second and third decades of the sixteenth century, Syria, Palestine, Egypt and Hungary were conquered. By the end of the sixth decade, Iraq, North Africa and Arabia were under the control of the Ottoman Turks. The Ottomans valued Jewish expertise in trade, manufacture, finance, administration and medicine. Consequently, Jews from Germany, Italy, Spain and Portugal arrived in Turkey. Other Spanish and Portuguese Jews went to Palestine. Safed in Galilee became a centre of Jewish learning and mysticism. The Middle East remained under Ottoman rule until the end of the First World War.

The Protestant Reformation brought its own troubles for the Jewish people. Martin Luther acknowledged in 1523 that they had been treated like dogs despite the fact that Christ was born a Jew. Twenty years later, when their conversion to Christianity failed, he denounced them viciously asserting that they should be enslaved or removed from Christian lands. The Counter Reformation also turned against them. The sixteenth century saw the establishment of ghettos in many European cities, particularly in Germany and Italy. The Spanish and Portuguese Inquisitions sought out secret Jews up to the seventeenth century. Many fled into Amsterdam which in the seventeenth century was a great centre of finance and trade. They became active in Holland's economy, especially that they were given religious freedom and protection. Holland and England were two enlightened countries at that time who accepted the Jews as valuable members of society and where the government did not meddle with their lives. Many Jews sought a living in the New World and settled in English, Dutch and French colonies.

The eighteenth and nineteenth centuries saw Jewish emancipation in most European countries. They were no longer regarded as outcasts, foreigners, aliens or a necessary evil, but citizens of the countries of their abode with equal rights and privileges before the law. A certain animosity toward them remained with the native peoples, generated by centuries of suspicion and hostility toward a people of a different culture. The Sephardim of France were favoured over the Ashkenazic Jews until 1789, the year of the revolution, when a National Assembly declared the freedom and equal rights of men. The Sephardim of southern France were granted full citizenship in 1790. Other countries followed suit. Holland granted its Jews full citizenship in 1795. French conquests in Italy and the Rhineland liberated the Jews in these lands. Napoleon Bonaparte presented himself as their liberator, but he discriminated against them in certain matters, favouring French peasants and Roman Catholic merchants. Frankfurt gave its Jews equal rights in 1811, the Prussian kingdom partial rights in 1812, but other German states took longer. There were riots against the Jews in Germany in 1819 and the 1830s saw large numbers of German Jews emigrating to the United States. Equal rights were granted to the Jews in the German states in the 1860s and confirmed by the German empire in 1871. Emancipation in Austria-Hungary was achieved in 1867, although religious freedom was granted in Hungary in 1850. The Italian Jews were emancipated in 1866 and the Rome ghetto abolished, while Switzerland granted its Jews full emancipation in 1874.

Most Polish Jews fell under Russian rule when Poland was partitioned in 1772 and 1795. Jewish merchants were forbidden to settle in central Russia in 1791. They were confined to certain territories in the early part of the nineteenth century and expelled from the villages in 1824 and from Kiev in 1827. Conscription into the Russian army was forced upon them until 1855. Organised attacks or pogroms against the Jews took place in Russia in 1881–1882 and in 1905–1907 and in the Ukraine in 1918–1920, and expulsion from Moscow in 1891. The largest number of Jews was found in Russia during the nineteenth century, but their emancipation did not take place until 1917 after the Bolshevik revolution. Herzl's *Der Judenstaat*, that is, The Jewish State, was published in 1869 and the first Zionist congress was held at Basle in 1897. Zionist activity was urgent for the establishment of a Jewish national home in Palestine. Stalin's oppression in the 1930s destroyed many Jewish intellectuals. The Nazis in Germany began their extermination of the Jews of Europe in the late 1930s with the eventual massacre of millions in central and eastern Europe in what is generally known as the Holocaust. The state of Israel was declared in May 1948.

The Holocaust attempted the extermination of the Jews of Europe. It was not the first of its kind, though it destroyed a larger number than any previous persecution. The massacres of 1096 by the Crusaders, of 1348–1349 at the time of the Black Death, of 1391 in Spain and of 1648–1667 in Poland had the same aim as the massacres by the Nazis. The gas chambers, ovens and human experimentation were of indescribable agony and horror, but so was the slaughter, the flaying, the roasting and the burning while alive. Although many Jews allowed themselves to be baptised when this facility was offered to escape torture and death, many preferred to die "for the sanctification of the Name", that is they sanctified God's name by remaining faithful to their God. When one considers the perseverance, resilience and capacity for survival of the Jewish people against unimaginable odds and attempts at their extermination; their pursuit of learning and preservation of their culture, their ingenuity in the generation of wealth and their excellence in most fields of life, one cannot help but have great admiration for such a people. Paul's words come to mind: "For I bear them record that they have a zeal of God, but not according to knowledge. For they being ignorant of God's righteousness, and going about to establish their own righteousness, have not submitted themselves unto the righteousness of God. For Christ is the end of the law for righteousness to everyone that believeth" (Ro.10:2–4).

Three major factors worked to keep Judaism alive despite extreme measures to exterminate the Jewish people. They were the Hebrew Scriptures, Rabbinical

Judaism and Messianism. The Scriptures were the foundation upon which rabbinical traditions and messianic aspirations were built. It is doubtful whether the latter two would have survived without the former. This is apart from the underlying reason that God preserved the Jews for their salvation and not, as some claim, for their role in the tribulation, Armageddon and the millennium.

Rabbinical Judaism preserved the culture and practices of the Jewish people. The Talmud enforced social segregation and discouraged spiritual or cultural assimilation into the non-Jewish systems of the nations amongst whom they lived. When the Karaite movement appeared toward the middle of the eighth century, it was regarded as a threat to Rabbinical Judaism and Jewish life. Karaism rejected the Talmud and insisted upon a literal adherence to the Bible with a stress upon the validity of personal interpretation. Karaism increased during the first four centuries of its emergence and was permitted to exist as another form of Judaism by Muslim rulers. The Jewish majority adhered to Rabbinical Judaism and this state of affairs persisted until this day. Both Karaites and Rabbanites longed for the termination of the exile, but the Karaites gave this matter a special consideration.

Messianism became prominent through messianic movements which appeared especially during times of persecution. Its basic ideas were of liberation and salvation in the kingdom of the messiah: a restored Davidic kingdom with a rebuilt temple. False messiahs arose from time to time. The first notable example was Simon bar Kosiba, known as Bar Kokhba, who rebelled against the Romans in Judea between 133 and 135 A.D. Other messiahs arose in the eighth century in Syria and Persia, in the twelfth century in Persia and in the thirteenth, fifteenth, sixteenth, seventeenth and eighteenth centuries in Italy, Spain,

eastern Europe and Palestine. One such was Shabbatai
Zevi, a native of Izmir (previously Smyrna) who
proclaimed himself messiah in 1665, at the age of thirty-
nine, in Gaza, Syria and Izmir and had a great following.
Like others before him, his claim ended in failure and
he converted to Islam in order to preserve his life. As the
Jewish people saw themselves still in exile under foreign
powers with the passing of the centuries, they began to
think of the time of the messiah as being in the distant
future, before the end of time. This idea has been carried
through by Christians who hold to the view that Christ
will effect a thousand years of peace when he will rule on
earth before the final cataclysmic end of human history.
Messianism was overtaken by political Zionism in the
nineteenth and twentieth centuries.

This brief history of the Jewish people concentrates
deliberately upon their persecution and dispersion, which
in the eyes of many, grants them the right to possess their
ancient land. They have been scattered in the world
without finding a permanent place that they could call
home and in which they could live according to their
beliefs and customs. It becomes obvious that the Zionist
movement strived to secure a sovereign state to which the
Jew knew that he belonged. He could then raise his head
in his own land and no longer be counted inferior in status
to any member of any nation upon earth. Unfortunately,
this was achieved by the dispossession of the Palestinian
Arab people of their land. A new situation was created
in which the Jewish state found itself on a constant war
footing. The Palestinian problem persists despite efforts to
achieve peace between Israel and its Arab neighbours.

The modern state of Israel was formed after two
thousand and five hundred years of Jewish dispersion.

Many Christians see this as a miracle. It is necessary to ask whether the Bible teaches that the land promised to Abraham four thousand years ago gives the Jews a divine right to lay claim to it today in fulfilment of that promise. Should Christians be involved in bringing the promise to fruition? Millions of Christians in the United States of America and others who follow the teaching of the Scofield Reference Bible in the United Kingdom and elsewhere will answer in the affirmative. This drives them inevitably to take the side of the Israeli people until Israel fulfils the purposes of God.

Biblical prophecy has engaged the minds of men beyond the realm of reason and common sense. An American journalist and author [see Bibliography (6)], described the role of militant American evangelists in their unrelenting support for Israel. The state of Israel in its complete form is necessary, in their view, for the return of Christ. The Temple must be built and animal sacrifices offered. This will be preparatory for the battle of Armageddon in the plain of Esdraelon, the biblical valley of Jezreel, southeast of Haifa, during which Christ will return to destroy the Antichrist and the enemies of the Jewish people. It is envisaged that four hundred million soldiers from China, Russia and countries neighbouring Israel will be involved in the battle. Those who hold such views seem to have forgotten that it needed two aeroplanes to drop atomic bombs on Hiroshima and Nagasaki to effect massive destruction. Two thirds of the Jews will be killed in the battle. Those who survive will have a favoured place during Christ's reign upon earth for one thousand years. The Christian Zionists believe that they must encourage things to happen in order to hasten the return of Christ. They favour nuclear proliferation and regard Russia as the great enemy. They think that events will start to happen during their lifetime, although they themselves would have been removed from earth by Christ before the dreadful tribulation and onslaught. In all this, modern interpreters have gone beyond their seventeenth to nineteenth century counterparts in England who favoured a Jewish return to Palestine without considering Jewish national sovereignty.

The interest of the Christian Zionist evangelists is political with a zeal for the fulfilment of their own brand of prophetic notions. Their objective is for Israel to possess its ancient land. Some include Iraq in their scheme. The Palestinians should be driven out and the Dome of the Rock and al-Aqsa mosques destroyed. They raise money for Israel that it may achieve the purposes of God. If, in the meanwhile, the oppression of a dispossessed people has to take place, then it cannot be helped. God is placed on the side of the oppressor, or rather becomes the instigator of oppression. The Bible is thus turned into a bigoted and nationalistic book. Some Arab Christians accept the doctrine of Israeli occupation of Arab lands as being divinely motivated. They see themselves as victims of a process beyond their control. They become uncertain as to where to place their loyalty and consequently take a neutral stance.

Another aspect of the subject is the view that states that the children of Israel never possessed the whole of the promised land. It is said that since God does not break his word, he will accomplish this in the millennium. The vast separation in time between the promise and its fulfilment means that only a small fraction of Abraham's descendants will inherit the promise while the majority would have turned to dust. It is not worth considering whether today's Jews are descended from Abraham or are proselytes or a mixed breed. It could be argued that God used the proselytes in order to give Abraham's descendants among them their ancient land.

The questions that must be addressed are these:

1. Why did God choose Abraham and his seed and give them a land?

2. Did the children of Israel possess the whole of the promised land?

3. Does the Bible teach that the Jews were to repossess the land of Israel at any time after the first coming of Christ?

4. Does the Bible teach that there will be a unique role for the Jews during the last seven years before a millennium?

5. Does Christ have to reign as king in Jerusalem for a thousand years?

The questions are closely related and cannot be discussed in complete isolation. It is hoped that the following chapters will do justice to the issues at hand.

BIBLIOGRAPHY

(1) Cecil Roth, A Short History of the Jewish People, (East and West Library, London, 1943).

(2) Israel Cohen, The Zionist Movement, (Frederick Muller, London, 1945).

(3) Solomon Grayzel, A History of the Jews, (The Jewish Publication Society of America, Philadelphia, 1948).

(4) Barnet Litvinoff, The Burning Bush, (William Collins Sons & Co. Ltd, London, 1988).

(5) Robert M. Seltzer, Jewish People, Jewish Thought, (Macmillan Publishing Co. Inc., New York, 1980).

(6) Grace Halsell, Prophecy and Politics, (Lawrence Hill & Company, Westport, Connecticut, 1986).

(7) Barbara W. Tuchman, Bible and Sword, (Macmillan Publishers Limited, London, 1983).

Chapter Two
Abram

The history of mankind from the creation to the call of Abram occupies eleven chapters in the Bible. The story of Abram and his descendants, including Jesus the son of David, covers the rest of the Bible. This is because God began to specify his plan of redemption in Abram, renamed Abraham, the father of all who believe (Gal.3:7) and in his progeny according to the flesh. The redeemer was to come from Isaac, not Ishmael; from Jacob, not Esau; from Judah, not his brethren; and finally from David, not his brethren. Mary, the mother of our Lord, was of the seed of David as was Joseph the husband of Mary. Jesus was therefore actually and legally the son of David. It is significant that Luke, in chapter three of his gospel, traces the genealogy of our Lord all the way back to Adam. He emphasises the unity of the human race by this and shows that Jesus is the central theme of the Bible and the one promised from the beginning to the whole of mankind. The Bible is not the history of nations divorced from the history of our Lord. The doctrine of the last days is not a set of prophecies of particular value divorced from the accomplishment of redemption to the full. The history of Abraham and his seed according to promise is the history of the Lord Jesus Christ culminating in his incarnation and work of redemption and the ingathering of the nations to himself.

The Ancient Historical Background of the Middle East

It is useful to give a brief account of the ancient history of the Middle East to show that the land of Canaan fell prey to many conquering nations in its long history. This fact has an important bearing upon the reason for God's gift of this particular land to Abraham and his seed.

God called Abram in Ur of the Chaldees in ancient Iraq. Ur was situated near the southernmost region of the Euphrates and the ancient shoreline. The shoreline extended farther north than the present position of the northern tip of the Arabian Gulf. Abram settled in Haran, a city in the north of ancient Iraq lying on a tributary of the Euphrates, the Balikh river, until his father died (Gen.11:31,32; 15:7). There was also a northern city of Ur (1), but Ur of the Chaldees is believed to refer to the city in the south.

The political climate of the Middle East was in a state of continuous flux and change. About 3100 B.C., more than one thousand years before the time of Abram, the Sumerian non-Semitic civilisation succeeded a Semitic civilisation in Iraq which may have originated in the Arabian peninsula. This earlier civilisation invented the first writing, which was developed by the Sumerians into the cuneiform, or wedge-shaped, writing (2)(3). Both civilisations preceded that of Egypt.

The Semites were the descendants of Shem the son of Noah. Genesis chapter 10 suggests that peoples such as the Akkadians, Amorites and Canaanites were descended from Ham. Archaeologists regard such as Semites. The concept of Semite in this regard is ethnic and not racial, based upon a similarity of language. The languages of the Akkadians, Babylonians, Assyrians, Canaanites, Chaldeans, Ethiopians, Aramaeans, Arabs and Hebrews seem to have originated from a common stem. Of these, the Arabic language is nearer to the Old Babylonian language of the nineteenth century B.C. than any other living language. There is a view among archaeologists and historians that the Arabian peninsula is the cradle of the Semites (4)(5)(6)(7)(8).

The Genesis account mentions cities which were not yet built after the Flood. With respect to Nimrod, for instance, it says: "And the beginning of his kingdom was Babel, and Erech, and Accad, and Calneh, in the land of Shinar" (Gen.10:10). Shinar was the land in ancient southern Iraq where Nimrod built his kingdom. The cities mentioned were established later in that area. In like manner, when the Bible says that Cain lived in the land of Nod (Gen.4:16), it means that he lived in the land which at a later time was called the land of Nod. Likewise, Abram pursued the kings of the east "unto Dan" (Gen.14:14) before his great grandson Dan was born and long before the tribe of Dan occupied the city in the north of Canaan which was called by his name. The Bible gives accounts of events written later than the time of their occurrence. It often identifies places by using their names at the time of writing. This principle will bear upon the interpretation of prophecy.

The Sumerians of the south of Iraq were organised into a civil system with an authoritative priesthood serving a multiplicity of gods. Ur was a city in Sumer. The Akkadians of central Iraq established a great empire about 2350 B.C., under Sargon I, the Great, with a central government and an army, long before the Greeks. The city state was the rule in ancient Iraq before Sargon, and in Greece until the conquest of the states in 338 B.C. by Philip, the father of Alexander the Great who is normally referred to as Philip of Macedon. Macedonia can be confused with the modern province of Greece, or the former Yugoslav province. Sargon diminished the authority of the priests in his realm. His empire and sphere of influence spread from the Lower Sea (the Arabian Gulf) to the Upper Sea (the Mediterranean). It included the Four Quarters of the known Earth of that day: Sumer in the south, Elam (Iran) in the east, Subartu in the north, reaching to the mountains of Turkey, and Amurru in the west as far as Syria and Canaan. The Akkadians did not destroy the civilisations they conquered, but absorbed their best features, while the army safeguarded property and trade throughout the realm. The Old Akkadian period ended around 2180 B.C. when it was destroyed by the Gutians, a non-Semitic nation of barbarians who came from the mountainous region of Iran and beyond. Gutian power lasted until 2070 when there was a resurgence of local culture and power for 110 years until the Elamites destroyed the city of Ur. The Amorites entered ancient Iraq from the west shortly after and also spread into Canaan. It is possible that during the times of the Elamite and Amorite invasions that Abram's family, and Abram in obedience to God's call, emigrated from Ur to Haran.

About the middle of the nineteenth century B.C. a great Babylonian empire was established under the rule of Hammurabi, an Amorite, best known for his code of communal, religious and national laws. His kingdom stretched from the Gulf to the Mediterranean and included Syria, Lebanon and Canaan. After the decline of this Old Babylonian kingdom about 1550, power shifted to the north where the Hurrians, the biblical

Horites whose home was in eastern Asia Minor (Turkey), established the kingdom of Mitanni, which encroached upon Hittite lands eastward and well into Syria (9). They were finally supplanted by the Hittites of Asia Minor whose empire was at its greatest between 1450 and 1200 (10). The Hittites conquered Babylon around 1600 (11) and spread into Syria by the fourteenth century. There is doubt whether the Hittite Empire existed at all. Velikovsky maintained that the Hittites were actually Chaldeans (12). When their empire dwindled in Asia Minor their states in Syria survived with Carchemish in the northeast on the Euphrates playing an important role. Carchemish was conquered by the Assyrians about the middle of the ninth century and finally annexed by them in 717 (13)(14). Meanwhile, the Aramaens controlled Syrian cities in the south including Damascus (15). They had entered Syria and ancient Iraq in the twelfth century during a recession in Assyrian power (16) and established themselves in Syria in the twelfth century. During the residence of the children of Israel in Canaan, the land was successively conquered by the Assyrians, Babylonians, Persians, Greeks and Romans. It was conquered by the Arabs, then by the Turks and finally ruled by the British until the formation of the modern state of Israel. Ancient Egypt also had its share of dominion over the land.

The land of Canaan formed the land bridge between the powerful countries in the east and Egypt. The Egyptians entered it from the south. Their influence goes back as far as the twenty third century. The geographical position of Canaan made it an object of conquest even by European powers in our twentieth century. It was subject to recurrent invasions in the past by the peoples who dominated the political scene. Armies marched upon its soil and battles were fought in its plains. It was divided at the time of

Abraham into small cities and settlements of peoples of different nations or tribes who often intermingled in one city. We read in Gen. 14:2 of five kings who met Amraphel, and his allies in battle in the region of the Dead Sea. The Canaanites did not form a national state, but remained divided. They had close relationships with Egypt during the Hyksos domination of Egypt and much of Canaan (1700–1550 B.C.). The Hyksos were a mixture of Semitic, Hittite and Hurrian peoples who originated mainly in Canaan. In order to protect their land after the Hyksos experience, the Egyptians attempted to rule over Canaan. Egyptian domination was established as far as Kadesh in Syria until the thirteenth century. The Egyptians battled with the Hittites, who retained control of the northern territories. Canaan remained a land of many peoples. The Philistines resided along the coastline in the south, the Hivites in the north well into Mount Lebanon, and in the hill country north of Jerusalem. The Amalekites lived in Sinai and roamed from the Negev to the borders of Egypt. There were also the nations mentioned in Gen.15:19,20. It was about 1450 B.C. that the children of Israel came out of Egypt and began their conquest of the land.

The Call of Abram

God's call to Abram came to him again in Haran after his father died. "Now the Lord had said unto Abram, Get thee out of thy country, and from thy kindred, and from thy father's house, unto a land that I will shew thee: and I will make of thee a great nation, and I will bless thee, and make thy name great; and thou shalt be a blessing: and I will bless them that bless thee, and curse him that curseth thee: and in thee shall all the families of the earth be blessed" (Gen.12:1–3).

The promise consisted of three elements. The first element, that God would make of Abram a great nation, referred to his progeny. He did not see the fulfilment of this. The promise was fulfilled primarily in the children of Israel. Ishmael also became a great nation and, to a lesser extent, Esau, who was Edom. A second fulfilment was in Abraham becoming the father of all who believe, albeit, a people formed from every nation.

The second element was personal. Abram would know material and spiritual blessings, his name would be great and others would be blessed through his friendship. This part of the promise was temporal in that it applied to Abraham during his lifetime. He was "very rich in cattle, in silver, and in gold" (Gen.13:2). He established his name when he pursued the invading kings, rescued Lot and was blessed by Melchizedek (Gen.14). Although he regarded himself as a stranger and a sojourner when he came to buy a plot to bury Sarah, the children of Heth (Hittites) said to him: "Thou art a mighty prince among us: in the choice of our sepulchres bury thy dead" (Gen.23:4–6). The name of Abraham is still great and is revered by Jews, Christians and Muslims.

Many interpret the words of blessing and cursing as referring not to Abraham only, but to the Jewish people. They quote examples from national and personal history to justify such a claim. A common statement is that Germany was defeated in the Second World War because of Hitler's destruction of the Jews. There is no justification for such an interpretation. The children of Israel were God's people in the Old Testament and he blessed them when they obeyed him, but delivered them to their enemies when they rebelled. God had a special relationship with them as he did with Abraham. This can hardly apply to the Jewish people after their rejection of Christ. Their role as a favoured people of God ended when the Lord was crucified. It is a gross exageration to suggest that God deals with people according to their relationship with Jews who reject his Son and stand against those of their kin who accept him. God's special people today are the true believers of Jews and Gentiles alike.

The third element of the promise concerned the blessing of the whole of mankind in the Lord Jesus Christ (Gal.3). We see here the connection between Abram's call and the plight of mankind since Adam's fall. God planned man's redemption through Seth, Noah, and Shem and narrowed the pathway of the fulfilment of the promise regarding the woman's seed (Gen.3:15), to Abram. The woman's seed was to conquer on behalf of those whom God had chosen from all nations, not from Abraham's progeny only. The blessing of mankind was God's ultimate objective: "And the scripture, foreseeing that God would justify the heathen through faith, preached before the gospel unto Abraham, saying, In thee shall all nations be blessed" (Gal.3:8). The making of a great nation of Abram must be seen in this light. It had no value of itself. God made Ishmael a great nation: he begat twelve princes (Gen.17:20). What purpose did that serve? The nation that was to be born of Isaac was to serve a mighty spiritual cause.

Why did God choose Isaac and not Ishmael? Ishmael was born according to a fleshly endeavour of a woman capable of conception. Abram believed God, that his seed will be innumerable and that mankind will be blessed in Christ when Sarai was beyond the age of conception (Gen.13:16; 15:5,6). God emphasised the necessity for faith, but also showed that the promise will be fulfilled in a manner which defied the natural order of things. "In the same day the Lord made a covenant with Abram, saying, Unto thy seed have I given this land, from the river of Egypt unto the great river, the river Euphrates: the Kenites, and the Kenizzites, and the Kadmonites, and the Hittites, and the Perizzites, and the Rephaims, and the Amorites, and the Canaanites, and the Girgashites, and the Jebusites" (Gen.15:18–21). The promise was specifically stated as being in the form of a covenant. The covenant was repeated in Genesis, chapter 17 and its basic significance revealed.

REFERENCES

(1) Jack Finegan, Light from the Ancient Past, (Princeton University Press, New Jersey, 1974), vol.1, p. 99.

(2) Jack Finegan, Archaeological History of the Ancient Middle East, (Westview Press Inc., Colorado; Wm. Dawson and Sons Ltd., Folkestone, 1979), pp. 17,18.

(3) Samuel Noah Kramer, The Sumerians, (The University of Chicago Press, Chicago, 1963), pp. 40,41.

(4) James Henry Breasted, Ancient Times, (Ginn and Company, Boston, 1944), pp. 136–139.

(5) Philip K. Hitti, History of the Arabs, (The Macmillan Press Ltd., London, 1982), pp. 9–11.

(6) Bernhard W. Anderson, The Living World of the Old Testament, (Longman Group UK Ltd., 1990), p. 34.

(7) Samuel Noah Kramer, ibid., p. 42.

(8) W. O. E. Oesterley and Theodore H. Robinson, A History of Israel, (Clarendon Press, Oxford, 1934), pp. 30,33.

(9) O. R. Gurney, The Hittites, (Penguin Books, Harmondsworth, Middlesex, 1981), p. 24.

(10) O. R. Gurney, ibid. pp. 29–31.

(11) O. R. Gurney, ibid. p. 24.

(12) Immanuel Velikovsky (Ramses II and His Time, Book Club Associates, London,1978.), pp. 140–179.

(13) O. R. Gurney, ibid., pp. 46,47.

(14) Peter James, Centuries of Darkness, (Jonathan Cape, London, 1992), p. 126.

(15) O. R. Gurney, ibid., p. 44.

(16) Peter James, ibid., p. 273.

Chapter Three
The Promised Land

The promised land was generally known as the land of Canaan. It was inhabited by a mixture of peoples and the Canaanites were found beyond its limits. The land was defined as being "from the river of Egypt unto the great river, the river Euphrates" (Gen.15:18). The Euphrates starts in the Anatolian mountains and flows through Turkey, Syria and Iraq. The river was to form the eastern arm of the northern border while the western arm was at the entrance to Hamath in Syria (Nu.34:8).

The River of Egypt

It is natural to imagine that the river of Egypt is the Nile. Gen.15:18 uses the same Hebrew word '*nahar*' for both rivers, but contrasts the river of Egypt with the Euphrates, which is called great. Yet the Nile is far greater than the Euphrates in its width and overall length. The word '*nahar*' *means river, but it can also mean current or stream or channel or watercourse*. The river of Egypt is mentioned in Nu.34:5 where the Hebrew word is '*nahala*' with the guttural 'h the letter 'het', and in other verses '*nahal*'. Both words mean river or rivulet or brook or stream or channel or watercourse or current or torrent or valley. All words are translated in various versions of the Bible as the "brook" or "wadi" of Egypt, 'wadi' being the Arabic word for valley. The river of Egypt is thought to be wadi el-'Arish (1)(2)(3). It runs from the central part of the Sinai Peninsula to the Mediterranean sea 90 miles east of Suez. A river flows through it in the rainy season. It was attributed to Egypt because Egypt was the dominant power over that land then.

Another interpretation regards the "river of Egypt" as the most eastern branch of the Nile in the Delta. This is incorrect since it places the land of Goshen within the boundaries of the promised land. Abram was told: "Thy seed shall be a stranger in a land that is not their's, and shall serve them; and they shall afflict them four hundred years...but in the fourth generation they shall come hither again" (Gen.15:13–16). They were to be strangers in Egypt until they are brought out of it "hither again" to possess the mount of the Amorites, its hills and plains, the land of the Canaanites and Lebanon, even to the Euphrates (Dt.1:7,8; 6:20–23). Thus, no part of Egypt was promised to Abram or his seed.

God identified the general boundaries of the land in Ex.23:31: "And I will set thy bounds from the Red sea even unto the sea of the Philistines, and from the desert unto the river", that is, from the gulf of 'Aqabah to the Mediterranean, and from Sinai in the south to the Euphrates in the northeast. Similar statements are made in Dt.11:24 and Josh.1:4 except that here the southern boundary is called the wilderness.

The Detailed Borders of the Promised Land

The boundaries of the land are outlined in Nu.34:3–15, while the inheritance of the tribes is detailed in Josh.15–19.

The description in Nu.34 and Josh.15 starts with the border of Judah in the south and proceeds westward, northward, eastward and to the south again. Starting from the southernmost part of the Dead Sea, the border stretched eastward south of the ascent of Akrabbim to the wilderness of Zin in the Negev, then southward to Kadesh-barnea near the borders of the Sinai desert and from there to the river of Egypt. This boundary included part of the wilderness of Paran into which the children of Israel entered after leaving the Sinai desert (Nu.10:12). Kadesh or Kadesh-barnea is thought to have been situated in today's plain of Qusaimah, where a spring, known as 'Ain el-Jadirat, often misnamed 'Ain el-Qudeirat, formed an oasis (4)(5)(6)(7). It is likely that 'Ain Qdeis, southeast of 'Ain el-Jadirat, represents the site of Kadesh more accurately as the name implies. It was from there that Moses sent men to spy the land (Nu.12:16; 13:1–3,25,26; Dt.1:19–22) and to the king of Edom (Nu.20:14). It was there that Miriam died. The river of Egypt formed the most western border and carried the border northward to the Mediterranean Sea. The land therefore included part of the Negev in its north and central portions and part of Sinai. It is worth noting that the major part of the Negev lying southeast from the Dead Sea to the gulf of 'Aqabah was not part of the promised land. The children of Israel passed there "through the way of the plain from Elath, and from Ezion-gaber" northward toward the wilderness of Moab (Dt.2:8). The plain was the Arabah or the 'Aravah in the Hebrew Bible, which stretched between the Dead Sea and the gulf of 'Aqabah. Ezion-gaber or Ezion-geber is situated in modern Jordan at the site of Tell el-Khalifah and belonged to Edom even though Solomon built his navy there (1Ki.9:26).

The Mediterranean Sea formed the west coast of the

promised land up to the south of Lebanon (Nu.34:6,7). The north border at this point formed a line drawn from the sea to Mount Hor. This is not Mount Hor in the south "by the coast of the land of Edom" where Aaron died (Nu.20:22–29). An eastern range of mountains runs from Arabia in the south to Lebanon and Syria in the north. North of al-Hijaz on the eastern side of the gulf of 'Aqabah stand the mountains of Midian. Seir lies north of this, and farther north, to the east of the Dead Sea, stand the mountains of biblical Moab, the high plateau of Gilead and the mountains of Bashan up to Mount Hermon. Hermon, between modern Lebanon and Syria, is part of this range of mountains which included Hor at the edge of Edom. A western range includes mountains in Syria, and in Lebanon the biblical Mount Lebanon, then the Carmel and the rest of the range of Israel's mountains. A coastal plain lies to the west in Syria and Lebanon and all the way to the south of Israel. It is not certain whether the northern Mount Hor belonged to the eastern or western range of mountains, but the association of its name with the southern Mount Hor may indicate that it belonged to the eastern range. The belt between the two ranges of mountains was formed by the Great Rift. It is thought that the earth's surface fractured with the consequent sinking of the land. The rift runs from Turkey, through Syria and the Beqa' valley in Lebanon and proceeds through the Jordan valley, the Dead Sea, the Arabah and the Red Sea to east central Africa as far as Malawi.

The border of the promised land continued northward from Mount Hor into Syria to the entrance of the district of Hamath, that is Hama of today. Hama lies on the river known as nahr el-Asi or the Orontes. The entrance was situated between the western and eastern range of mountains. The border would have had to pass through south Lebanon and the Beqa' valley to reach Hamath. The coastal plain, with Tyre, Sidon and other cities, did not form part of the land. There is no mention of the border reaching the Euphrates. If it had done so, it would have marked the area where the river makes its great bend in Syria, not as far as Carchemish. The border at the Euphrates would have been narrow. The eastern border then went to the city of Zedad – modern Sadad, southeast of Homs, then to Riblah where Nebuchadnezzar judged Zedekiah and the nobles of Judah at a later time (2Ki.25:6; Jer.39:5,6; 52:9–11), then descended to the Sea of Chinnereth or Lake Tiberias, and along the Jordan River to the Dead Sea (Nu.34:11,12) where it joined the border of Judah. A significant part of south and east Lebanon and a significant part of Syria would have fallen within Israel's borders. If modern Israel were to regain these boundaries it would have to expand into south and east Lebanon and well into northern Syria.

The details of the inheritance of the individual tribes are found in Josh.15–19. Added to this was the land given to the tribes of Reuben, Gad and half the tribe of Manasseh to the east of the Jordan. Half of Gilead, the whole of Bashan east of Lake Tiberias and north of the Yarmuk River which pours into the Jordan, and as far as Mount Hermon, was given to Manasseh. The other half of Gilead was given to Reuben and Gad (Dt.3:12–16).

The River Jabbok is today's nahr ez-Zarqa in Jordan, having its source near 'Amman, the biblical Ramoth-ammon. Its deep valley formed the natural northern boundary of Ammon (Nu.21:24; Dt.2:37; 3:16; Jg.11:13). Its course was southwestern and divided Gilead before flowing into the Jordan River 30 miles north of the Dead Sea. The River Arnon – known today as wadi Mujib – formed the southern border of Ammon and the northern border of Moab (Nu.21:13; Jg.11:13). It flowed into the Dead Sea about its middle part. The southern boundary of Moab was the River Zered. The land of Edom lay south of Moab. The Amorites wee dispossessed of Gilead by Manasseh (Nu.32:39–42). Golan, a city in Manasseh, was given to the Levites (Josh.21:27). Midian lay along the eastern coast of the gulf of 'Aqabah. To the north, therefore, was Edom, then Moab, then Ammon, although Ammon was situated farther inland to the east. Edom, the land of Esau, Moab and Ammon, the lands of the children of Lot, were not parts of the promised land (Dt.2:5,9,19). Heshbon, modern Hasban, lay south of the Yarmuk River. It belonged to Moab, but was captured by the Amorite king Sihon who made it his capital before it was given to the tribe of Reuben (Nu.21:26; Josh.13:15,17).

No mention of the Euphrates is made in the division of the land among the tribes. The matter may have been left to rest temporarily because the tribes received land east of the Jordan River beyond the originally designated borders. Manasseh's lot reached well into Syria. Even so, when the land was partly conquered, Josh.21:43 says: "And the Lord gave unto Israel all the land which he sware to give unto their fathers; and they possessed it, and dwelt therein." This means that the tribes must have reached the Euphrates and that they must have occupied part of each region of their land. The land was to be conquered piecemeal, lest it became depopulated, because of the policy of extermination of its inhabitants which was commanded by the Lord (Ex.23:29,30; Dt.7:22–24). Its full conquest came about in the days of David and Solomon.

REFERENCES

(1) Jack Finegan, Light from the Ancient Past, (Princeton University Press, New Jersey, 1974), vol. 1, map 3, p. 138.

(2) Hasting's Dictionary of the Bible (T & T Clark, Edinburgh, 1963), p. 236.

(3) R. L. Ottley, A Short History of the Hebrews to the Roman Period, (Cambridge University Press, 1924), p. 96.

(4) Hasting's Dictionary of the Bible, ibid., p. 546.

(5) John L. McKenzie, Dictionary of the Bible, (Macmillan Publishing Company, New York, 1965), p. 471.

(6) Jack Finegan, ibid., p. 152.

(7) The Archaeological Encyclopedia of the Holy Land, edited by Avraham Negev, (Thomas Nelson Publishers, Nashville, Tennessee, 1986), p. 2.

Chapter Four
The Occupation of the Promised Land

There are two views held by many Bible students regarding Israel's reoccupation of its ancient land. One view is that Israel never occupied the whole extent of the promised land and its conquest must be fulfilled in the future. The modern state of Israel is the beginning of this process. Another view is that even if Israel occupied the land after the Exodus, it must reoccupy it. The reason for this is that the Jewish people have to be re-established as a nation in their land to enable or facilitate the return of Christ (1)(2). This view is generally held by premillennialists, who believe that when the Lord returns he will establish a kingdom on earth, centred on Jerusalem, which will last a thousand years.

Some argue that God's promise of the land to Abram was twofold. One promise considered the land between the river of Egypt and the Euphrates (Gen.15:18), while another considered the land of Canaan (Gen.17:8). They say that Joshua allotted Canaan to the tribes, but not the land of Gen.15:18. The latter will be given to Israel in the millennium (3)(4). A further argument points out that Abraham, Isaac and Jacob did not possess the land in its entirety and will therefore possess it after Christ's return. If this argument is taken to its logical conclusion, it must hold true of all of Abraham's seed from his day until the end of time. That a millennial possession was intended by God's promises to the patriarchs (Gen.26:3; 28:13) has no foundation in Scripture or in common sense. Would God promise them the land they walked upon only to exercise his favour after thousands of years? Even eternal life for the believer begins upon earth (Jn.17:3).

The naivety of the millennial argument is clear when God's timetable is considered. God said of Abraham's seed that they would be bondslaves – in Egypt – until he brings them back to Canaan (Gen.15:13–21). The Exodus was therefore the beginning of the fulfilment of their possession.

God called Moses to deliver the people out of Egypt in order to dispossess the nations of Canaan and made mention of the more powerful nations (Ex.3:8,17). It is said repeatedly that the Lord was bringing them to the land which he swore to their fathers to give them (Ex.13;5,11; 23:23; 34:11). When God was angry with Israel in the desert because of their sin, Moses reminded him of his promise to their fathers to multiply their seed and give them the land for ever (Ex.32:13; Nu.11:12; Dt.26:15). God said, go up "unto the land which I sware unto Abraham, to Isaac, and to Jacob, saying, Unto thy seed will I give it…and I will drive out the Canaanite, the Amorite, and the Hittite, and the Perizzite, the Hivite, and the Jebusite" (Ex.33:1,2; Dt.1:7). When God showed Moses the land, he said: "This is the land which I sware unto Abraham, unto Isaac, and unto Jacob, saying, I will give it unto thy seed: I have caused thee to see it with thine eyes, but thou shalt not go over thither" (Dt.34:4). "And the Lord gave unto Israel all the land which he sware unto their fathers" (Josh.21:43–45). It is, therefore, certain that the possession of the land after the Exodus was in fulfilment of God's promises to the patriarchs. His timetable was for that time, not for the twentieth century or the millennium.

The Exodus and the Conquest of the Land

"And it came to pass in the four hundred and eightieth year after the children of Israel were come out of the land of Egypt, in the fourth year of Solomon's reign over Israel, in the month Zif, which is the second month, that he began to build the house of the Lord" (1Ki.6:1). This is the surest record of the time of the Exodus and places it about 1450 B.C. or a little earlier. Some have equated the Exodus with the expulsion of the Hyksos from Egypt around 1580. This view is incorrect, because the Hyksos were masters over the Egyptians, not their slaves. Others prefer a date between 1350 and 1260. Their argument is based upon Ex.1:11: "And they built for Pharaoh treasure cities, Pithom and Raamses". Because of these names many authors give a later date for the Exodus (5)(6)(7)(8)(9)(10). They argue that the writer of 1Ki.6:1 reckoned twelve generations of priests from Aaron, allowing forty years for each generation. There is no indication that the writer did this. It can be argued, on the other hand, that the treasure cities were so named at the time of writing of the scroll, a frequent practice in the Bible. Archaeological evidence supports the existence of a city at the site of Jericho in the early part of the fifteenth century, but not a century later. Further, Genesis 47:11 says of Joseph that he gave his family "a possession in the land of Egypt, in the best of the land, in the land of Rameses." The spelling of Rameses in the Hebrew Bible is the same as Raamses in Exodus 1:11. Both words have the same letters in the correct order. A good discussion of the subject is given by

Robinson (11). He concludes: "But in any case the date of the Exodus can hardly have been later than the early part of the fifteenth century" (12). The late periods shorten the time of Joshua and the Judges considerably. It spanned at least four centuries until the reign of Saul. This can be confirmed by adding the years in the book of Judges. Further, the children of Ammon claimed the land once possessed by Sihon and the Amorites from the hand of Jephthah. Jephthah asked them why they did not recover the contested cities during the previous three hundred years (Jg.11:26). Paul said, "And after that he gave unto them judges about the space of four hundred and fifty years, until Samuel the prophet" (Acts 13:20). The cities were occupied by Israel a short time after the invasion of Canaan. Another century passed between the time of Jephthah and the reign of Saul.

The children of Israel defeated the Amorite kings Sihon and Og and possessed their land east of the Jordan before they crossed over. The land from the Arnon River to Mount Hermon became the possession of Gad, Reuben and half of the tribe of Manasseh (Nu.21:21–35; 32:33–42: Dt.3:3–17). The land of the Ammonites was farther east from Sihon's kingdom between the Arnon and Jabbok rivers. It was not dispossessed (Dt.2:19,37).

The disobedient nation which came out of Egypt perished in the wilderness except for Caleb and Joshua. Joshua led the invasion, which started north of the Dead Sea, with the fall of Jericho. Jericho was a fortified city and commanded the route from the east to the west of the Jordan and other routes leading to central Canaan. Ai fell next. The five Amorite kings, who rallied against the Gibeonites for surrendering to Israel, ruled over Jerusalem, Hebron (Arabic, Al-Khalil), Jarmuth (modern Khirbet el-Yarmuk or Tell Yarmut), Lachish (Tell ed-Duwair) and

Eglon (Tell el-Hesi or Tell Hasi). Eglon commanded the route between Jerusalem and Gaza. Joshua defeated the kings and took their land (Josh.10). The king of Gezer came to the aid of the king of Lachish and was also defeated. Joshua took Libnah (Tell Buran) also and Nakkedah. The cities were all situated in land allotted to Judah except for Gezer which was allotted to Ephraim and became a city of refuge (Josh.21:21). Israel thus occupied the hill country with its valleys and plains. The song of Deborah suggests that the tribe of Dan occupied land by the sea, as did Asher (Jg.5:17). Joshua extended his conquest in the south to Kadesh-barnea and to Goshen in Judah. He then proceeded north to Gaza and farther to Gibeon (El-Jib), (Josh.10:40,41). Hebron was given to the Levites; its fields and villages to Caleb (Josh.14:13,14; 1Chr.6:55,56).

The conquest of Galilee in the north is related to the deeds of Jabin, king of Hazor (Tell el-Qadah or Tell Hazor), five miles southwest of Lake Huleh. Jabin gathered a number of northern kings to fight Israel (Josh.11:1–3). Their cities were Madon, west of the Sea of Chinnereth or Lake Tiberias, Shimron (Tell Shimron) in upper Galilee, Achshaph (Tell Regev) northeast of Shimron toward Acco, while Dor was on the Mediterranean coast to the south of Haifa. Jabin rallied the kings north and south of Tiberias, the Canaanites to the east and west, the Hittites, Amorites, Perizzites and Jebusites in the mountains and the Hivites under Mount Hermon. The kingdoms included the plain of Jezreel running southeast from Mount Carmel. Jabin's plan was to wage a major war to stop Joshua from conquering the north country. Joshua was victorious in battle and chased the kings as far as Sidon in the west and Mizpeh by Mount Hermon in the east (Josh.11:8). He burnt the city of Hazor and later gave it to the tribe of Naphthali (Josh.11:10; 19:36). A summary of the conquest is given in Josh.11:16–23. The hills and the south country refer to Judah including the Negev and its part adjoining Mount Seir or Edom to the east. Josh.11:17, which says: "Even from the Mount Halak, that goeth up to Seir, even unto Baal-gad in the valley of Lebanon under Mount Hermon", means that the country from south to north was conquered, including a portion in the Beqa' valley in Lebanon. Another summary is given in Josh.12, which includes the conquest of cities in the west country. "So Joshua took the whole land, according to all that the Lord said unto Moses; and Joshua gave it for an inheritance unto Israel according to their divisions by their tribes. And the land rested from war" (Josh.11:23).

Joshua lived 110 years (Josh.24:29). When he was old, the Lord said that there was much land to be possessed, "now therefore divide this for an inheritance unto the nine tribes, and the half tribe of Manasseh" (Josh.13:1–7). This indicates that there was a resurgence of strength among the nations of Canaan and reoccupation of some land. Hazor, for instance was recaptured by the Canaanites who reclaimed it as their capital before it fell again by the hand of Barak (Jg.4:2,23,24). There were also the Philistines (Josh.13:2), although no battles are recorded between them and Joshua. It would appear that the conquest was not consolidated and there was much work to be done. Judges 1 details the cities taken by the various tribes of Israel among whom the people of the land lived.

The period of the Judges was a period of great unrest. The Lord left the nations to prove Israel, "five lords of the Philistines, and all the Canaanites, and the Sidonians, and the Hivites that dwelt in mount Lebanon, from mount Baal-hermon unto the entering of Hamath" (Jg.3:3). The children of Israel failed, not only in driving the people of the land out, but in intermarrying with them and serving their gods. The Lord raised their enemies against them. There were battles with the Midianites, Amalekites, Ammonites, Moabites, Philistines and even with Cushan-rishathaim of Mesopotamia into whose hands the Lord sold them (Jg.3:5–8). Dan was reduced to two towns, whereupon they conquered Laish in the north of Canaan and called it Dan (Jg.18). Canaan was under the control of the Philistines in the days of Samson. The struggle with the Philistines continued in the days of Saul and David. David reigned for forty years (1Chr.3:4), from about 1012 to 972 and Solomon for forty years after (2Chr.9:30), from 972 to 932.

It is not necessary to recount the details of David's and Solomon's conquests. The conquest of Jerusalem was an important event. It was situated in Benjamin (Jg.1:21) on the border with Judah. When David became king, he moved against the Philistines in the valley of Rephaim, south of Jerusalem, defeated them, but they returned, only to be defeated again (2Sam.5:17–25). The establishment of David's kingdom is recorded in 2Sam.8 and 1Chr.18:1–14. The Philistines were subjugated as were the neighbouring lands. David prevailed over Edom where he left a garrison, and over Moab, so that the Edomites and Moabites became his servants. He subdued the Amalekites in the Negev and the Ammonites in the east, and extended his kingdom to Hamath and the Euphrates (2Sam.8:3) and placed garrisons in Damascus. He also defeated the Syrians when they confederated with the Ammonites against him (2Sam.10; 1Chr.19:1–19). Geshur, a Syrian kingdom to the east of the Sea of Chinnereth remained a sovereign kingdom (2Sam.13:37). David had married the king's daughter of whom Absalom was born (2Sam.3:3). David's kingdom therefore included the whole land from the Euphrates to the Sinai Peninsula, besides other lands to the east of the Jordan belonging to Edom, Moab and Ammon. He also destroyed the power of the Philistines in his day.

1 Kings 4 records how Solomon placed officers to collect victuals for his household from the cities in his realm. Cities are mentioned along the Mediterranean coast which included previous Canaanite and Philistine strongholds and cities in the valley of Jezreel and along the west bank of the Jordan River. "And Solomon reigned over all the kingdoms from the river" – the Euphrates – "unto the land of the Philistines, and unto the border of Egypt: they brought presents, and served Solomon all the days of his life" (1Ki.4:21). After the dedication of the Temple, "Solomon held a feast, and all Israel with him, a great congregation, from the entering in of Hamath unto the river of Egypt" (1Ki.8:65). He collected tribute from "all the people that were left of the Amorites, Hittites, Perizzites, Hivites, and Jebusites" (1Ki.9:20,21). He "numbered all the strangers that were in the land of Israel" (2Chr.2:17). It can be said with certainty that the whole of the promised land and its peoples were subdued during the reigns of David and Solomon (13)(14).

It is plain from this account that it is incorrect to state that the children of Israel conquered Canaan only and not the land from the river of Egypt to the Euphrates. They conquered even more than was promised when the regions east of the Jordan River are included. Nehemiah, who lived when Judah was a province of the Persian empire, confirms God's faithfulness. His prayer mentions God's covenant with Abraham "to give the land of the Canaanites, the Hittites, the Amorites, and the Perizzites, and the Jebusites, and the Girgashites, to give it, I say, to his seed, and hast performed thy words; for thou art righteous" (Neh.9:7,8). The fact that other nations lived in their cities during the reigns of David and Solomon does not alter the principle of their subjugation. Such has always been the case with conquering kingdoms and empires. The conquered peoples may have been thinned, but not utterly displaced or destroyed. The Romans ruled over Palestine, but the inhabitants of Palestine were largely non-Roman. The British ruled over India, but India was still inhabited by its own people. They ruled over Palestine by a mandate, but Palestine was inhabited by Arabs and Jews while the British were a minority. The French ruled Algeria and the Italians ruled Libya in the twentieth century, but these lands remained inhabited by their own people. When the Egyptians, or Assyrians, or Babylonians, or Persians, or Arabs subjugated Palestine, they did not replace the people by their own. A partial exception was made in the case of Samaria by its Assyrian conqueror who brought in peoples from other conquered lands. (2Ki.17:24; Ezra 4:10). It is enough that Solomon exercised dominion over the conquered lands; that he made the vanquished his servants and collected tribute from them and that he left the way open for the Israelites to settle wherever they wished.

The Nations of Genesis 15:19–21 and their Fate

Further evidence that Israel had dominion over the promised land is obtained from the fate of the nations of the land.

The political system in Abraham's day consisted of scattered settlements and cities with chieftains who governed one single town or village. The inhabitants were organised into cities in Joshua's day with kings ruling over large areas at times.

The **Kenites** were nomads, kinsmen of the Midianites. They lived in the south of the country. Jethro, also called Hobab, father-in-law to Moses, was the priest of Midian and a Kenite (Ex.2:16; 3:1; Jg.1:16). He was acquainted with the desert and guided the children of Israel through it. Moses said to him, be to us "instead of eyes" (Nu.10:31). The Kenites lived amidst the Amalekites in the Negev. Before Saul attacked the Amalekites, he warned the Kenites to get out from among them, because they showed kindness to Israel in the desert (1Sam.15:6). Heber the Kenite, of the children of Hobab, left his clan to live in the district allotted to Naphthali. He was on good terms with Jabin, king of Hazor, whose city was situated northeast of Safed. It was his wife Jael who killed Sisera, Jabin's captain (Jg.4:11,18–21). Some Kenites lived in the towns of Judah, while others of the house of Rechab became scribes. They were the Tirathites, the Shimeathites and the Suchathites (1Chr.2:55). They were absorbed into Judah.

The **Kenizzites** were named after Kenaz, son of Eliphaz, son of Esau (Gen.36:11,15). Caleb and his brother Othniel are called Kenezites (Nu.32:12; Josh.14:6,14; 15:17), although they were descended from Judah (1Chr.4:13–15). The Hebrew Bible spells Kenizzites and Kenezites the same way. The Kenizzites lived in Edom and in land allotted to Judah. Those who lived in Judah were absorbed into Israel.

The **Kadmonites** were said to have descended from Kedemah, the son of Ishmael (Gen.25:15; 1Chr.1:31), although the promise to Abraham was made before Ishmael was born. The Kadmonites lived in Kedemoth near the Arnon river. Their city was given by the Reubenites to the Levites (Josh.13:18; 21:37; 1Chr.6:79).

The **Hittites** were the sons of Heth, son of Canaan, son of Ham (Gen.10:1,6,15). They are said to have established an empire reaching as far back as 1800 B.C. in the region of Turkey and Syria. It extended as far as Babylon at one time. Hamath, and later Carchemish on the Euphrates, and Aleppo were Hittite cities. Syria was called by the Assyrians and the Chaldeans the land of Hatti and was regarded as land of the Hittites in Josh.1:4, where it says, "this Lebanon even unto the great river, the river Euphrates, all the land of the Hittites." Carchemish was conquered by Sargon II in 717 and Hamath in 720 (2Ki.18:34; 19:13; Is.10:9). Velikovsky thought that the Hittites were Chaldeans and that no Hittite empire ever existed, nor was it ever mentioned by Greek historians (15).

The Hittites had settlements in the land of Canaan in the days of Abraham. Hebron was such a place, where they were called "the people of the land". Sarah died there and was buried in the cave of Machpelah, which Abraham bought from Ephron the Hittite (Gen.23:2,7,12,19,20). They also dwelled in the mountains (Nu.13:29). The Canaanite Hittites were dispossessed, but not exterminated. They intermarried with Israel, as did Solomon later on (Jg.3:5,6; 1Ki.11:1) and as did Esau at the beginning (Gen.26:34; 36:2). Abimelech and Uriah, both Hittites, were David's men (1Sam.26:6; 2Sam.11:6). The Hittites remained in northern Syria for about two centuries after Solomon and their rulers were called "kings of the Hittites" (1Ki.10:29; 2Ki.7:6; 2Chr.1:17).

The **Perizzites** were regarded with the Canaanites as inhabitants of the land in a general way (Gen.13:7; Jg.1:4).

Their name is said to indicate that they lived in the open country in unwalled villages. The children of Joseph complained to Joshua that their portion was small. He gave them the mountainous country where the Perizzites lived (Josh.17:14–18). It appears that many of them lived in Ephraim and Judah. The men of Judah conquered those in their midst (Jg.1:4).

The **Rephaim** were conquered by Amraphel in Abraham's day. Their kings were kings of the East and lived in Ashteroth Karanaim, the Ashtaroth of Bashan where Og king of the Amorites reigned (Gen.14:5; Josh.12:4; 13:12). The name Rephaim may have referred to their gigantic stature rather than to their ethnic origin. Og himself was "of the remnant of the giants" and his land, "the land of the giants" (Dt.3:11–13) was inherited by Manasseh. They lived mainly on the east side of the Jordan River. The Moabites displaced those in their midst and called them Emim (horrors), while the Ammonites called them Zamzummim (howlers), (16) and also displaced them (Dt.2:10,11,19–21). The rest of the Rephaim lived west of the Jordan in the land of Ephraim (Josh.17:15). The valley of the Rephaim, south of Jerusalem between Ephraim and Judah, was named after them. When the Philistines invaded Judah they camped in this valley (2Sam.5:18,22; 23:13; 1Chr.11:15; 14:9) and were defeated by David (2Sam.5:25).

The **Amorites** were of the sons of Canaan (Gen.10:16). They were known as far back as 2300 B.C. when they were called Amurru by Sargon I of Akkad. They came from the region of Syria, entered ancient Iraq some 300 years later, ruled many famous cities and spread into Canaan. They were at their acme in Lebanon and Syria about 1500, but were finally conquered by the Hittites – or Chaldeans –around 1300. Being the most powerful nation in Canaan, they were at times regarded as the people of the land (Gen.15;16; 48:22; Jg.6:10).

The Amorites lived in several regions in Canaan. Those in the south were in Hazezon-tamar or Engedi (2Chr.20:2) at the western shore of the Dead Sea and as far as Akrabbim in the south (Jg.1:36). They were in Hebron where Abraham had friends among them, having lived in the plain of Mamre the Amorite (Gen.14:7,13; 13:18). They also inhabited the mountains during the Israeli conquest (Dt.1:7,20). The Gibeonites, who made peace with Israel through a deception, were of the Amorites, but became "hewers of wood and drawers of water" (Josh.9). Five Amorite kings who warred against the Gibeonites for their desertion were defeated by Joshua (Josh.10:5).

Kings Sihon and Og were kings of the Amorites on the east coast of the Jordan. Their kingdoms included Gilead in the south and Bashan in the north as far as Mount Hermon. The two kingdoms were divided between Manasseh in the north, then Gad, then Reuben in the south (Nu.32:33–42; Dt.3:1–7; Josh.13:7–12,29–32). The land of the Amorites west of the Jordan fell to Benjamin, Judah, Simeon and Dan.

The **Canaanites** were descendants of Canaan, son of Ham. Their cities were along the coast from Sidon to Gaza and in the Jordan valley, in contrast to the Amorites of the mountains (Gen.10:15–19; Nu.13:29; Dt.1:7; Josh.5:1). Their land was allotted to Manasseh (Josh.17:12; Jg.1:27), Ephraim, Zebulun, Asher and Naphthali (Jg.1:28–33). They were not driven out completely, and their idolatry was a constant threat to the children of Israel.

The **Girgashites** were descended from Canaan (Gen.10:16). They are repeatedly mentioned with the nations of the land (Dt.7:1; Josh.3:10; 24:11). They lived on the west side of the Jordan and were conquered by Joshua.

The **Jebusites** lived in the central range of mountains in the region of Jerusalem (Nu.13:29; Josh.11:3; 15:8,63; 18:16). Jebus or Jerusalem was their city (Jg.19:10,11) until it was captured by David (2Sam.5:6,7; 1Chr.11:4–7). Melchizedek, king of Salem in Abraham's day (Gen.14:8) and Adoni-zedec, at the time of Joshua (Josh.10:1), were kings of Jerusalem.

It is necessary to say a little about the Philistines although they are not mentioned with the nations of Gen.15:19–21. They are regarded in the Bible as the sons of Ham, of whom came Mizraim "and Casluhim, (out of whom came Philistim,) and Caphtorim" (Gen.10:13,14; 1Chr.1:12). They were the "remnant of the country of Caphtor" (Jer.47:4). The Lord said: "Have not I brought up Israel out of the land of Egypt? and the Philistines from Caphtor" (Amos 9:7). Most writers believe that Caphtor was Crete and that the Philistines came from there and from the southwest of Asia Minor about 1200 B.C., after the Trojan war (17–25). They base their view upon the writing of Raamses III who repelled the Peleset (Philistines) and the Peoples of the Sea about that time. They were prevented from settling in Egypt and settled in Canaan instead. Grave doubt is placed upon this theory by an able scholar, Velikovsky, who maintained that such events took place some 800 years later and did not concern the Philistines, but the Persians (26). Jewish tradition equates Caphtor with Cyprus. Those who believe that the

Philistines came about 1200 tend to regard the biblical account as anachronistic. They mean that the Philistines were placed in a historical context during which they could not have been there. An invasion of Canaan by the Philistines in 1200 does not negate the possibility of earlier settlers reaching the land.

There was a Philistine settlement in the south of Canaan in Abraham's and Isaac's days. Abraham at Beer-sheba, and later Isaac, made a peace covenant with Abimelech of the Philistines (Gen.21:22–34; 26:26–31). It is interesting that Abimelech is a Semitic name, meaning father of the king. The Philistines formed a small settlement in those days. An important verse, Ex.13:17, says: "And it came to pass, when Pharaoh had let the people go, that God led them not through the way of the land of the Philistines, although that was near; for God said, Lest peradventure the people repent when they see war, and they return to Egypt." The way of the land of the Philistines was along the Mediterranean coast from Egypt and would have taken the people a few weeks to traverse it. The verse suggests that the Philistines were at war with the people of Canaan at the time of the Exodus. This may indicate that they came in successive waves. We do not read of Joshua fighting with them, yet they were in the land when he was an old man (Josh.13:2,3). They were a force to be reckoned with in the days of the Judges and of David. Ginzberg says of the Philistines in the days of David: "In no sense were they descendants of those Philistines who had concluded a treaty with Isaac; they had emigrated from Cyprus at a much later date" (26). Perhaps those supplemented the existing Philistines through a new invasion.

REFERENCES

(1) Hal Lindsey, The Late Great Planet Earth, (Marshall Pickering, Basingstoke, England, 1988), pp. 42,43.

(2) David Baron, The Visions and Prophecies of Zechariah, (Hebrew Christian Testimony to Israel, London, 1951), p. 492.

(3) Charles C. Ryrie, Basic Theology, (Victor Books, Wheaton, Illinois, 1987), pp. 455–457.

(4) Arthur W. Kac, The Rebirth of the State of Israel, (Marshall, Morgan & Scott, London, 1958), pp. 22–25.

(5) Bernhard W. Anderson, The Living World of the Old Testament, (Longman Group UK Limited, 1990), pp. 646,647.

(6) Gaalyah Cornfeld and David Noel Freedman, Archaeology of the Bible: Book by Book, (Harper & Row, San Francisco, 1976), p. 36.

(7) Jack Finegan, Light from the Ancient Past, (Princeton University Press, New Jersey, 1974), pp. 72,117–121.

(8) Kathleen M. Kenyon, Archaeology in the Holy Land, (Methuen & Co. Ltd., London, 1979), p. 205.

(9) Werner Keller, The Bible as History, (Book Club Associates, London, 1956), p. 121.

(10) John L. McKenzie, Dictionary of the Bible, (Macmillan Publishing Company, New York, 1965), p. 257.

(11) W.O.E. Oesterley & Theodore H. Robinson, A History of Israel, (Clarendon Press, Oxford, 1934), vol. 1, pp. 71–80.

(12) Oesterley & Robinson, ibid., p. 80.

(13) F.F. Bruce, Israel and the Nations, (The Paternoster Press, Exeter, 1978), p. 32.

(14) H.C. Leupold, Exposition of Isaiah, (Baker Book House Company, Grand Rapids, Michigan, 1988), p. 11.

(15) Immanuel Velikovsky, Ramses II and His Time (Book Club Associates, London, 1978), pp. 140–179.

(15) Oesterley & Robinson, ibid., vol. 1, p. 32.

(16) Bernhard W. Anderson, ibid., pp. 76,129.

(17) The Archaeological Encyclopedia of the Holy Land, edited by Avraham Negev, (Thomas Nelson Publishers, Nashville, Tennessee, 1986), pp. 295,296.

(18) Cornfeld and Freedman, ibid., pp. 84–87.

(19) Jack Finegan, ibid., pp. 121,135.

(20) Kathleen M. Kenyon, ibid., pp. 207,212.

(21) Werner Keller, ibid., pp. 169–174.

(22) John L. McKenzie, ibid., pp. 672,673.

(23) Dictionary of the Bible, Original Edition by James Hastings, Revised Edition, (T&T Clark, Edinburgh, 1963), p. 765.

(24) Robert M. Seltzer, Jewish People, Jewish Thought, (Macmillan Publishing Co. Inc., New York, 1980), p. 19.

(25) Immanuel Velikovsky, Peoples of the Sea, (Book Club Associates, London, 1977).

(26) Louis Ginzberg, The Legends of the Jews, (The Jewish Publication Society of America, Philadelphia, 1987), vol. 4, p. 94.

Chapter Five
The Exile and After

When Solomon built high places for the gods of the heathen, God raised Hadad the Edomite and Rezin the Syrian against him (1Ki.11:14–25). Rezin occupied Damascus. The Kingdom was divided after Solomon's death. Rehoboam, Solomon's son, ruled over Judah and Benjamin in the south, while Jeroboam ruled the northern tribes of Israel. There were wars between Judah and Israel for 150 years, and civil war in Israel between Tibni and Omri (1Ki.16:21,22). The aid of foreign powers was sought by the conflicting parties against their brethren. Ben-hadad aided Asa of Judah (reigned 913–873) against Baasha of Israel and occupied some of his cities (1Ki.15:16–20). These were later regained by Ahab (1Ki.20:34). Hazael of Syria (836–786) took the eastern possessions of Reuben, Gad and Manasseh in Gilead and Bashan in the days of Jehu king of Israel (2Ki.10:32,33). He also took Gath from Jehoash of Judah and was bought off from taking Jerusalem (2Ki.12:17,18). "He oppressed Israel all the days of Jehoahaz" (2Ki.13:22). But Jehoash, son of Jehoahaz regained the cities which Hazael took, from Ben-hadad, Hazael's son (2Ki.13:25). Azariah of Judah, also known as Uzziah (786–736), 2Ki.14:21; 2Chr.26:1) captured some cities from the Philistines while the Ammonites sought his favour (2Chr.26:6–8). Edom had revolted from the hand of Judah earlier. Although Jehoram (849–842) smote them in battle, the Edomites remained in a state of rebellion (2Chr.21:8–10). There was war between Israel and Judah in the days of Joash of Israel (800–785) and Amaziah of Judah (804–775). Joash destroyed the walls of Jerusalem (2Ki.14:13). Jeroboam his son (785–745) was king over Israel during the latter years of Amaziah and a contemporary of Uzziah. "He restored the coast of Israel from the entering of Hamath unto the sea of the plain", that is the Dead Sea and took Damascus (Dt.3:17; 2Ki.14:25,28).

Jeroboam's conquest did not last long. Assyria began to expand its empire shortly after. Tiglath-pileser (745–727) captured cities in the north of Israel as far down as Naphthali and also took Damascus in the Days of Pekah, king of Israel (2Ki.15:29; 16:9). He carried captives into Assyria. Samaria, capital of Israel which was built by Omri, fell to Shalmaneser in 722 in the days of Hoshea. He carried most of the people into captivity and replaced them by peoples from Babylon, Assyria and northern Arabia (2Ki.17:3–7,24). These intermarried with the remnant of Israel and their progeny were the Samaritans. The northern kingdom of Israel was obliterated by Assyria. The reason for the captivity was that the people departed from the Lord (2Ki.17). Sennacherib (705–681) came against Judah and took its fenced cities in the days of king Hezekiah (2Ki.18:13; Is.36:1), but failed to take Jerusalem. Judah remained a kingdom until it fell under the Babylonian yoke more than a century after Israel's fall.

Assyria was destroyed by an uprising of Babylonians and Medes in 612 B.C. The Chaldeans of Babylon were the next empire builders. The power of Syria had been broken and the kingdom of Israel no longer existed to be a barrier between Judah and the new conquerors from ancient Iraq. The Babylonians ventured against Judah twice in the days of Jehoiakim. Daniel was one of the captives of the first campaign under Nebuchadnezzar (605–562) (Dan.1:1–6). Marauding bands of Chaldeans, Syrians and Ammonites troubled Judah during the seventh year of the reign of Jehoiakim (601 B.C.). Nebuchadnezzar destroyed all Egyptian influence from the river of Egypt to the Euphrates (2Ki.24:7). He besieged Jerusalem in 589 during the eighth year of Jehoiakin, son of Jehoiakim. Both father and son did evil in the sight of the Lord. Nebuchadnezzar "carried away all Jerusalem, and all the princes, and all the mighty men of valour, even ten thousand captives, and all the craftsmen and smiths: none remained, save the poorest sort of the people of the land". He made Jehoiakin's uncle, Mattaniah, a vassal king in Jerusalem and changed his name to Zedekiah (2Ki.24:14–17). When Zedekiah rebelled, Nebuchadnezzar returned and took Jerusalem in 586. Zedekiah was blinded, chained and led to Babylon and his sons were slain (2Ki.25:1–7). Five years later, Nebuchadnezzar came for the last time against Jerusalem and burnt the house of the Lord (Jer.52:29,30). The rest of the people were led into captivity, apart from the poor who were left to cultivate the land (2Ki.25:8–21). Such was the fate of the great monarchy of David and Solomon. It started with intertribal warfare in the divided kingdom and wars with local enemies. There were victories and defeats, land lost and land regained, but, generally, the land possessed by the children of Israel diminished. Finally, Israel was led captive to Assyria and Judah to Babylon some 135 years later. The end result was disastrous for the people of God. They rebelled against him and were dispossessed. Foreigners lived in their land with the poor who were left behind by their powerful conquerors.

The Return from Exile

The exile lasted until 536 B.C. Babylon fell to the Persians shortly before this. Cyrus, king of the Persians, issued a decree for the return of the captives from Assyria in the north and Babylon in the south. Those who returned were committed to the building of Jerusalem and the house of the Lord. About 50,000 returned (Ezra 2:64,65; Neh.7:66,67), mainly from Judah and Benjamin and Levi. Many captives from Israel remained in Assyria. The Temple was built in the days of the Mede Darius I (the Great), who reigned from 521 to 486. The walls of Jerusalem were rebuilt under the supervision of Nehemiah in the days of Artaxerxes (465–423). The political condition of the Jews at that time was summed up in Nehemiah's prayer: "Behold, we are servants this day, and for the land that thou gavest unto our fathers to eat the fruit thereof and the good thereof, behold we are servants in it. And it yieldeth much increase unto the kings whom thou hast set over us because of our sins: also they have dominion over our bodies, and over our cattle, at their pleasure, and we are in great distress" (Neh.9:36,37).

There were two positive results of the exile: the people were reunited into one nation and they no longer worshipped idols. They remained under Medo-Persian rule until Alexander defeated the Persians. His successors became masters of the Jewish people, first, the Ptolemies of Egypt, then the Seleucids of Syria. There was a period of Judean independence under the Maccabees from 167 to 63 B.C. Pompey captured Jerusalem for the Romans in 63. The Herodians reigned under Roman suzerainty from 37 B.C. The Jews remained under Roman domination until the Temple was destroyed in 70 A.D. They were then dispersed throughout the known world for nineteen centuries until the modern state of Israel was established in 1948.

Chapter Six
The Alleged Necessity for Modern Israel

When the Jews began to return to Palestine in large numbers in the twentieth century and the state of Israel was declared in 1948, many Christians saw the fulfilment of biblical prophecy regarding God's ancient people. There was a Puritan movement in the seventeenth century that worked for the return of the Jews to England, from which country they were expelled by Edward I in 1290 A.D. The purpose of this was to complete their dispersion and effect their conversion, then, with England's help, they could be resettled in Palestine. It was held that these things were essential for the return of Christ: the prophecies concerning the Jews had to be accomplished. The notion that the Jews should become a sovereign nation in Palestine was not considered. Lord Shaftesbury in mid-nineteenth century England was energetic in carrying the idea of the resettlement of the Jews forward. This was coupled with the voice of Jewish writers and thinkers in Europe who worked to awaken the zeal of their people to seek a country. As Jewish emancipation in Europe took place and political Zionism emerged, Britain found itself the hand which could bring about the settlement of the Jews in Palestine, due to its political influence in that land.

Another movement, known as Dispensationalism, was

introduced in England by John N. Darby around 1830 and was adopted by the Scofield Reference Bible. It divides history into seven stages or dispensations during which certain principles of life and conduct are placed upon man by God. The seventh dispensation is that of the kingdom of Christ in the millennium. While all dispensationalists are premillennialist in their belief – anticipating a thousand year rule of Christ upon earth – not all premillennialists are dispensationalists. American Christians have expanded the subject and opinions vary regarding many questions. Will the tribulation before the millennium involve Christians? When will the Rapture – the removal of Christians from earth by Christ – occur? When will believers and unbelievers be resurrected? What is the role of the Jews, converted and unconverted, in all this? The common denominator underlying the various schemes is the absolute necessity for the Jews to be established in their ancient land. Christ cannot return before this happens. The major ideas of this subject will be discussed in the following chapters.

It will be shown in chapter ten that the ultimate reason for God's election of Abraham and his seed and their settlement in Canaan was to ensure the incarnation of Christ. Premillennialist ideas go beyond this and find reasons for God's election in the role of the Jews at the end of the age.

One view holds that 144,000 Jews will be converted a little prior to the beginning of a seven year period of dreadful tribulation before the Lord's return. They will be sealed by the Holy Spirit on their foreheads and made indestructible, being capable of surviving nuclear explosions and natural calamities. Their task would be to evangelise the world. The "great" multitude which no man could number, of all nations, and kindreds, and people, and tongues" of Rev.7:9, would be the product of their efforts. They will more than make up for their earlier failure to preach the gospel (1).

This view cannot be substantiated and is mere speculation. The tribe of Dan is omitted from the 144,000 (Rev.7:4–8) and it is conjectured that this may be due to the appearance of the Jewish antichrist or false prophet out of that tribe. The tribe of Ephraim is also omitted. If an innumerable number of people is saved through the Jewish endeavour, how is it that the earth remains in the grip of evil and men do not repent despite the havoc of the tribulation? (Rev.9:20,21, 16:11).

Some hold that the Jews will fulfil their mission of converting the Gentiles during the millennium (2). This notion is based upon the words of Amos 9:11,12 and its interpretation by James in Acts 15:13–17: "As it is written, After this I will return, and will build again the tabernacle of David, which is fallen down; and I will build again the ruins thereof, and I will set it up: that the residue of men might seek after the Lord, and all the Gentiles, upon whom my name is called, saith the Lord." It is said that the church age will cease after Chris's return, the Jews will be converted (Ro.11:25,26) and Israel will fulfil her final destiny of converting the rest of the Gentiles.

This view cannot be deduced from the words of James. James said: "Simon hath declared how God at the first did visit the Gentiles, to take out of them a people for his name. And to this agree the words of the prophets; as it is written...". That is, the entrance of the Gentiles into the faith through Peter was a fulfilment of the prophets. The tabernacle of David, with the word of the Lord, priesthood and kingdom, was rebuilt through the Lord Jesus Christ in his offices as prophet, priest and king. The church would preach the gospel, as Peter did, and the residue of men, the Gentiles would seek the Lord then, not in the millennium. It would be a hard thing to suggest that James misread the prophets and expected a literal restoration of David's kingdom in the millennial age. James demonstrated an important principle in biblical interpretation. The Messianic concepts in the Old Testament are spiritualised without expecting a physical fulfilment. It has been said that every Old Testament prophecy concerning the Lord was fulfilled literally. This is true with respect to his birth, ministry, death and resurrection, but not with respect to the concepts behind these things. His kingdom was spiritual and he rebuilt David's tabernacle spiritually. The Lord was not literally anointed with oil, nor did he serve as high priest in the Temple at Jerusalem. He was the only high priest from the tribe of Judah and he offered the supreme sacrifice once and for all in the temple of his body.

There is no salvation for anyone after the Lord's return. The promise regarding the election of the Gentiles was to be fulfilled from the time of the Lord's ministry "unto the end of the world" (Mt.28:20). The Lord commissioned his disciples to preach the gospel to every nation and sent the Holy Spirit to enable them to do this. He was born to be "a light to lighten the Gentiles" (Lk.2:32; Acts 26:22,23). When Jesus withdrew himself from the multitude it was "that it might be fulfilled which was spoken by Esaias the prophet saying"…"And in his name shall the Gentiles trust" (Mt.12:15–21; Is.42:4). This is verified by Paul's word to the Jews, after he quoted Is.6:9,10, "Be it known therefore unto you, that the salvation of God is sent unto the Gentiles, and that they will hear it" (Acts 28:25–28). The Gentiles always had a share in the kingdom of God. God was to pour his Spirit "upon all flesh" and whosoever shall call on the name of the Lord shall be delivered" (Joel 2:28,32). Isaiah's prophecy shows the universal aspect of salvation throughout its pages. Let it not be forgotten that the promise of a saviour in the garden of Eden was made, not to the Jews, who did not exist then, but to mankind. The election of Abraham was the means by which God accomplished his redemption to men and women from every nation. It is a speculation of the greatest degree to suggest that the remnant of the nations will be converted after the return of Christ.

The confusion about these matters arises from two things: a distorted view of the kingship of Christ and a distorted view of his return. Both cases give the Jewish people a role which they no longer have. The Old Testament era served its purpose and was dissolved by the advent of Christ, never to be re-established. The kingship of Christ will be discussed in the remainder of this chapter.

The Kingship of Christ

God promised David that he would establish his house and kingdom for ever (2Sam. 7:12–16; 1Chr.17:11–15; Ps.89:3,4,28–36). It is said that the kingdom will be political in nature over the children of Israel and not over all men (3). "According to Jeremiah 30:9, the people of Israel who serve with David their king will be resurrected at the beginning of the millennial reign of Christ" (4). The verse says: "But they shall serve the Lord their God, and David their king, whom I will raise up unto them", although raise up does not mean to raise from the dead, but to bring to power. The author says that David and Christ will reign over Israel in the millennium, but Christ's rule will be universal also (5). There will thus be two persons upon one throne, each having the authority of that throne. Jeremiah chapter 30 has nothing to do with the millennium. It tells of God's gracious intention to bring back his people from the Babylonian captivity. They were afflicted for their iniquity (v.15), but God would punish their oppressors (v.16), a clear reference to the Medo-Persian conquest of Babylon. It is a common thing in the Old Testament, and an important principle to know, that when God's people are in the doldrums and God promises a future blessing, he speaks of the restoration of their land with all the associated blessings, the destruction of their enemies and, usually, a promise regarding the Messiah and his kingdom. Images from the past are used to describe the future in a manner which the people could understand. When Jeremiah spoke of David reigning over Israel, as did Ezekiel, (37:24), the reference was to Christ, David's son, the branch that would grow up unto David (Jer.23:5; 33:15).

The verses in Jer.33:14–17 promise the Branch of righteousness when Judah shall be saved and Jerusalem shall dwell safely and "David shall never want a man to sit upon the throne of the house of Israel." It is said: "Again, there is no justification to interpret this in any other sense than to understand its fulfilment as being subsequent to the second coming of Christ in the kingdom on earth" (6). But should one remove a portion of Scripture from its immediate context? Verse 18 continues the narrative: "Neither shall the priests the Levites want a man before me to offer burnt offerings, and to kindle meat offerings, and to do sacrifice continually". If verses 14–17 refer to the millennial kingdom, so must verse 18. It follows that the Levitical priesthood, with its animal sacrifices, will be reinstated in the kingdom. The millennial political kingdom, thus, has two kings sitting on one throne, while Christ the king allows sacrificial animals to be slain for

God's pleasure. This is nothing but a return to the law and the bondage of Egypt. It is the inevitable consequence of minds that cannot differentiate between passages in the Bible which demand a literal fulfilment from those which demand a spiritual fulfilment. Besides, all the references to the Lord as the Branch concern his first coming. There is nowhere in the Old Testament a reference to the Lord's second coming. A further error in the millennial explanation is to equate a thousand years with eternity. A thousand years must end, but for ever does not. But if the passage under consideration refers to Christ's spiritual kingdom, then it involves believers, who offer spiritual sacrifices, for Christ "hath made us kings and priests unto God" (Rev.1:6; Ro.12:1; 1Pet.2:5).

What was God's timetable for the kingship of Christ over Israel? Was it to follow his incarnation and continual reign in heaven and in the hearts of men, or was it to follow his second coming?

The promise of a child in Is.9:6,7 is associated with his high status and everlasting kingship upon David's throne. This is said to be political and not spiritual, as Mary's understanding of the matter was when the angel spoke to her (Lk.1:30–33) (7). If Mary thought that her son was to become a political king, she would have expected him to achieve this during his lifetime on earth. As he was to be the saviour during his life, he was to be king also. As he was to be the prince of peace on earth, he was to sit on David's throne. The promise was related directly to his birth and not to many centuries later.

When the wise men from the east sought the king of the Jews, even Herod knew that this meant the Messiah. The one who was to be born in Bethlehem was to be the Governor of God's people by virtue of his birth and not in some distant future (Micah 5:2). He entered the capital riding the colt of an ass (Zech.9:9; Mt.21:4,5, etc.), "as it is written, Fear not, daughter of Sion: behold thy King cometh, sitting on an ass's colt" (Jn.12:15). He agreed with Pilate that he was a king, but his kingdom was not of this world (Jn.18:36,37). It was spiritual, within believers (Lk.17:21), a kingdom of "righteousness, and peace, and joy in the Holy Ghost" (Ro.14:17). The accusation over his cross was extremely significant and was recorded in all the gospels: "THIS IS JESUS THE KING OF THE JEWS" (Mt.27:37; Mk.15:26; Lk.23:38; Jn.19:21). It was written in Greek, Latin, and Hebrew (Luke 23:38), the languages of the day in Israel. The matter was settled by Peter who said of David "that God had sworn with an oath to him, that of the fruit of his loins, according to the flesh, he would raise up Christ to sit on his throne." He goes on to show that Jesus did sit on the right hand of God and was made both Lord and Christ (Acts 2:30–36). In other words, the promise that he would sit on David's throne was fulfilled absolutely, for he is "the root and the offspring of David" and has "the key of David" (Rev.22:16: 3:7).

It is a feeble excuse and an insult to say that since the Jews rejected Christ, he will try again at a future date, or that the kingdom was shelved until the millennium. Though the majority rejected him, the early believers were all Jews, as were the three thousand who were converted on the day of Pentecost.

The notion that the kingship of Christ was to be political falls to the ground because the Lord ran away from establishing a political kingdom (Jn.6:15). His disciples lacked understanding even after his resurrection, and men and women make the same mistake today. The disciples had not learnt to stop asking about times and seasons and expected a political kingdom. It is naive to say the Lord did not answer them, therefore their question must stand. The Lord was not a 'yes' or 'no' man in his answers, which often seemed irrelevant to the question but were always pregnant with truth which went beyond what was being asked. The Lord's answer was very precise. It is as if he said: Stop thinking of a political kingdom of Israel: my kingdom is a worldwide spiritual kingdom which expands through the preaching of the gospel by the power of the Holy Spirit (Acts 1:6–8). When the disciples were filled with the Holy Spirit, there was no further talk of Israel's kingdom in their theology. The matter was laid to rest for ever. They knew that a political Israel had no part in God's plan, but that believers belonged to the kingdom, for the Father "hath translated us into the kingdom of his dear Son" (Col.1:13). Had Christ sat as king in Jerusalem for ever, would he have suffered the death of the cross? Would he have been a victorious or a vanquished king?

Since the Son reigns eternally as the second person in the Holy Trinity, the question arises: why should he receive a kingdom, as though he had none? Is it a greater honour to sit on an earthly rather than a heavenly throne?

Christ, as the mediator between God and man, redeemed those whom the Father had given him, by his own blood. He must be able to save and preserve them until they are glorified and like David, to work for their good. None of them must perish, but all must be brought into that spiritual kingdom which increases through the spread of the gospel, like the wheat which grows and ripens and the mustard seed which forms a bush and the leaven which leavens the dough. The Lord received all authority and power and sent the Holy Spirit to ensure the salvation of his people. This mediatorial kingship of Christ is usually disregarded by those who seek an earthly throne for him. A millennial kingdom is introduced forcibly where it should have no existence. "But of the Son he saith, Thy throne, O God, is for ever and ever: a sceptre of righteousness is the sceptre of thy kingdom" (Heb.1:8). Christ, as the spiritual king and priest of his people reigns for ever (Heb.5:6; 6:20; 7:17). Their presence in heaven will always be based upon their relationship to him. But, as keeper of his people upon earth, he must be the king who controls the destinies of nations for the benefit of his own. When the Lord was on earth, he gave up for a while that which belonged to him. The Father was in charge, while the Holy Spirit, who indwelt the Lord, enabled him to carry out his task. When the Lord rose from the dead, he sat on the Father's right hand having received authority to rule the world for the good of the church. "The LORD said unto my Lord, Sit thou at my right hand, until I make thine enemies thy footstool" (Ps.110:1). Christ confronted the Jews of his day with this promise about himself (Mt.22:24; Mk.12:36; Lk.20:43). The theme was taken up by Peter when he applied it to Jesus (Acts 2:32–36). The writer to the Hebrews applied it twice (Heb.1:13; 10:13). Similarly, Paul wrote of Christ's exaltation and of the power and authority which he received above every name that is named to be the head of the church and that to him every knee should bow (Eph.1:20–22: Phil.2:8,9). This universal kingship as mediator will have served its purpose when all enemies are put under his feet. "The last enemy that shall be destroyed is death". Then he will deliver the kingdom to the Father (1Cor.15:24–28) and exercise the kingship which is his by right as the Son of God.

Christ sat on the throne of David as the spiritual king of his people. He sat on the Father's right hand as king, and is the king of the church and of the world now.

REFERENCES

(1) Hal Lindsey, There's A New World Coming, (Harvest House Publishers, Eugene, Oregon, 1984), pp. 83,100–104,108–111,151,186.

(2) Arthur W. Kac, The Rebirth of the State of Israel, (Marshall, Morgan & Scott, London, 1958), pp. 364–369.

(3) John F. Walvoord, Major Bible Prophecies, (Zondervan Publishing House, Grand Rapids, Michigan, 1991), p. 100.

(4) Ibid., p. 102.

(5) Ibid., p. 104.

(6) Ibid., p. 103.

(7) Ibid., p. 105.

RECOMMENDED READING

Barbara W. Tuchman, Bible and Sword, (Macmillan Publishing Limited, London, 1983).

Louis Berkhof, Systematic Theology, (The Banner of Truth Trust, Edinburgh, 1984), pp. 406–411.

Chapter Seven
The Great Disjunction

Two approaches are used by interpreters of biblical prophecy in discovering the future of the Jewish people. The first involves the collection of verses concerning Israel, without heeding their historical context, and their interpretation in a haphazard manner. It is said, for example, that since the land of Canaan was promised to Abraham and his seed for ever, the promise was not fulfilled because they possessed it intermittently and temporarily. The fulfilment will take place during the millennial reign of Christ on earth. But, should Abraham and his seed be raised from the dead and made possessors of the land for one thousand years, it could not be said that they possessed it for ever.

This kind of thinking neglects the conditional aspect of God's dealing with man which depends upon man's moral state. When God promises to bless a people, he is not obliged to fulfil his promise without taking account of their moral state. "At what instant I shall speak concerning a nation, and concerning a kingdom, to pluck up, and to pull down, and to destroy it; if that nation, against whom I have pronounced, turn from their evil, I will repent of the evil that I thought to do unto them. And at what instant I shall speak concerning a nation, and concerning a kingdom, to build and to plant it; if it do evil in my sight, that it obey not my voice, then I will repent of the good, wherewith I said I would benefit them" (Jer.18:7–10). Jonah's mission to Nineveh illustrates this principle. Jonah pronounced the destruction of the city, but knew in his heart that if the city repented God would not destroy it, as indeed happened. God's constant pleading with the children of Israel through the prophets was that they might turn from their evil ways and escape disaster. David understood this principle regarding his house and kingdom (2Sam.7:12–16). He said to Solomon before he died: "That the Lord may continue his word which he spake concerning me, saying, If thy children take heed to their way, to walk before me in truth with all their heart and with all their soul, there shall not fail thee (said he) a man on the throne of Israel" (1Ki.2:3,4). God did not establish the kingdom of David's children when they disobeyed him, but sent them into captivity.

The second approach in discovering Israel's future deals with the matters of the end of time. It is the premillennialist and dispensationalist view, taught by the Scofield Reference Bible and a multitude of commentators, although it is nowhere mentioned in the New Testament. Its foundation is the presence of the Jews as a sovereign nation in the promised land. The idea is derived from Daniel 9:24–27. Both approaches are complementary and can be regarded as parts of a major whole. The second approach will be dealt with in this chapter.

The Excavation of Time

It is said that a seven year period of tribulation is approaching during which the battle of Armageddon will be fought and Christ will return then to set up his earthly kingdom and effect the conversion of the Jews (1)(2). These in turn will fulfil their mission of the conversion of the Gentiles (3). When the end result is said to be a mere 144,000 converted Jews, with none from the tribe of Dan or Ephraim, the prospect looks bleak for the Jewish people. The promises would not have touched the majority, who died with the passing of the years.

The restoration of the Jews as a sovereign nation in their ancient land, before the start of the seven year period, is said to be essential for their role. There is no reason for this to be the case, nor is there a connection between the conversion of the Gentiles and Jewish sovereignty. God ensured the incarnation of his Son and the entrance of the Gentiles into the kingdom through the preaching of the Jewish apostles when the Jews were under the rule of Rome. It is said also that their return to their homeland would be the beginning of the fulfilment of the Lord's words: "When ye shall see these things, know that it is near, even at the doors" (Mt.24:33), although the Lord was speaking of the destruction of the Temple (5). The Lord's parable of the fig tree (Mt.24:32) is discounted totally as a parable and the fig tree is regarded as a symbol for Israel (6). 1948, the year of the formation of the modern state of Israel, is taken as the starting point for a count which will span a generation and which will end in climactic events (7) during the last seven years. The Lord's words in Mt.24:34 define the time when such things will occur: "This generation shall not pass, till all these things be fulfilled." It is asked: "What generation? Obviously, in the context, the generation that would see the signs – chief among them the rebirth of Israel. A generation in the Bible is something like forty years. If this is a correct deduction, then within forty years or so of 1948, all these things could take place. Many scholars who have studied Bible prophecy all their lives believe that this is so" (8). Now, since 1948+40 = 1988, the time has come and gone without the possibility of the expected events taking place. The deduction of the writer and the views of the scholars who have studied Bible prophecy all their lives are obviously incorrect. The rebirth of Israel was not hinted at or mentioned as a sign in the Lord's discourse. The Lord was talking about the generation of men and women who heard his words. Despite this, men and women proceed to give their insights into new facets of the same mould. Some give themselves more leeway and say that a generation is equivalent to man's life, that is 70 or 80 years.

The Lord's discourse about the siege of Jerusalem and his return is interpreted in the light of a misunderstanding of Dan.9:24–27. Events which have been fulfilled are still awaited.

Daniel 9:24–27 reads: "Seventy weeks are determined upon thy people and upon thy holy city, to finish the transgression, and to make an end of sins, and to make reconciliation for iniquity, and to bring in everlasting righteousness, and to seal up the vision and prophecy, and to anoint the most Holy. Know therefore and understand, that from the going forth of the commandment to restore and to build Jerusalem unto the Messiah the Prince shall be seven weeks, and threescore and two weeks: the street shall be built again, and the wall, even in troublous times. And after threescore and two weeks shall Messiah be cut off, but not for himself: and the people of the prince that shall come shall destroy the city and the sanctuary; and the end thereof shall be with a flood, and unto the end of the war desolations are determined. And he shall confirm the covenant with many for one week: and in the midst of the week he shall cause the sacrifice and oblation to cease, and for the overspreading of abominations he shall make it desolate, even until the consummation, and that determined shall be poured upon the desolate."

The Hebrew Bible says seventy sevens, without specifying the length of each seven. The premillennialist argument asserts that the seventieth seven will not follow the sixty-ninth seven consecutively. There is a great gap or parenthesis from the ending of the sixty-ninth week or 483rd year until the beginning of the seventieth week, the time being from the death of Christ until our generation. This is nothing less than an excavation of time. A big hole is created which spans centuries and disrupts the normal highway of time. The explanation given is that the cutting off of the Messiah – Christ's death – and the coming of the people of the prince –the destruction of the Temple in 70 A.D. – are said to occur after the sixty-ninth seven or 483 years, but not in the seventieth seven. Since the Temple was destroyed 37 years after the death of Christ, that is 30 years longer than seven years, the indication "is that there is a time period between the end of the 483 years and the beginning of the final 7 years" (9). It is plain that this is neither an argument nor a logical conclusion, but a contrived concept which must be utterly rejected. One writer agrees that the long gap between the 69th and 70th weeks "is not explained, or even hinted at in Daniel's revelation concerning the seventy weeks. For this reason Israel, and even the early church before the destruction of Jerusalem, had no way of knowing about, much less understanding, that highly significant truth" (10). This implies than Christians today have more understanding of biblical prophecy than the apostles. Why not put the matter in another form and say that neither the Lord nor his apostles knew anything of this crucial long gap? The writer proceeds to prove his case for the long gap, unsuccessfully, by stating the premillennialist doctrine of eschatology, without giving any justification for it (11). It is like the Arabic proverb which says: "He explained what water is, after a long effort, by saying it is water". One cannot prove a point by using its assumed consequences as its own proofs.

Dan.9:24 states that seventy sevens are determined to fulfil five things which must fall within this period and not twenty centuries later. They are the finishing of transgression and of sin, the making of reconciliation for iniquity, the bringing in of everlasting righteousness, the sealing up of vision and prophecy (Hebrew, prophet), and the anointing of the most Holy. It is bizarre that anyone should doubt that these things refer to the Lord Jesus Christ and his earthly ministry. "He appeared to put away sin by the sacrifice of himself" (Heb.9:26; 1Jn.3:5), "blotting out the handwriting of ordinances that was against us" (Col.2:14). "God was in Christ reconciling the world unto himself, not imputing their trespasses unto them" (2Cor.5:19; Heb.2:17). God sent forth Christ Jesus "to declare his righteousness for the remission of sins that are past" (Ro.3:25). "Grace will reign through righteousness unto eternal life by Jesus Christ our Lord" (Ro.5:21). He is made unto us righteousness (1Cor.1:30; 2Cor.5:21). "Righteousness shall be the girdle of his loins" (Is.11:5). He was the Holy one who was anointed by the Holy Spirit (Lk.1:35; 4:18; Acts 4:27; 10:38; Heb.1:9; Jn.3:34), not the millennial temple of Ezekiel 40–43, or of the New Jerusalem (12). There is no want of verses in the Bible to confirm these matters which do not belong to a future millennial age (13). Even the millennium will not be sin free as most premillennialists affirm. Christ will rule with a rod of iron because of prevailing sin, until the nations engage in war against Christ when Satan is loosed.

What of the sealing of vision and prophet? Vision and prophet are not defined by the article 'the' in the Hebrew Bible. Daniel and his prophecy are not the object of the sealing, but vision and prophet in general. Vision was the predominant means by which God spoke to the prophets, whether in waking visions or visions of the night. The sealing is said by premillennialists to relate to the second advent of Christ, claiming that the vision will not be understood until the time of its fulfilment approaches. This is why the early church had no idea what Daniel was talking about. But the verse does not mean to keep the vision and prophecy closed and dark until the time of their fulfilment. Nor does the sealing carry the meaning of stamping or verifying the truth of a document. The Lord's tomb was sealed that it may not be opened. A scroll was copied and sealed when its contents were completed, that nothing be added or taken away from it. In other words, Old Testament type of prophecy and vision would cease, having fulfilled their role with the coming of the Messiah. "For all the prophets and the law prophesied until John" and "the law and the prophets were until John: since that time the kingdom of God is preached" (Lk.16:16; Mt.11:13). The gospel age had arrived: Old Testament visions and prophets ended with John, although the Apostles of the Lord saw visions and some Christian men, as seen in the books of Acts and Revelation. The word of God came to men through his incarnate Son by direct communication. The dreams and visions prophesied by Joel were fulfilled on the day of Pentecost by the outpouring of the Holy Spirit upon the disciples. Their response could not have been other than understanding the gospel and declaring it. The book of Revelation and the visions of Peter and

Paul seem to be an exception (Acts 10; 16:9). But the apostles cannot be placed in the same category as Old Testament prophets. Their visions were not regarding Messiah's redemptive work which was the real burden of the Old Testament. They guided the early church in breaking new ground for the gospel. The Book of Revelation was written to comfort the persecuted church, and to tell how God will make the whole world his own by conquering all the evil in it, not to foretell the details of our age and the end of time.

Seventy sevens cannot mean an unlimited or indefinite time. If an employee is told that he shall be made redundant in three months, should he understand that after two months there will be an indefinite period before the redundancy takes effect? If a builder is told that according to his contract, he has to take down the scaffolding, complete the decorations and clear the rubbish in seven weeks, should he imagine that after six weeks he has two or three years before the seventh week comes into effect? Such bending of the meaning of words is done to allow an interpretation to fit a certain scheme. Dan.9:24–27 would be a deathblow to the premillennialist concept of the future if its events have been fulfilled already. The Lord's discourse in Mt.24; Mk.13; and Lk.21 will have to be reinterpreted. The seven years following a long gap are a cornerstone for those who interpret the Book of Revelation in a literal manner. It is clear that verse 24 is Messianic entirely, having been fulfilled during the first advent of Christ two thousand years ago.

The seventy sevens began with the commandment or word regarding the restoration and building of Jerusalem. In order to fit their pattern of years, premillennialists start the count in the year 445 B.C., when Artaxerxes gave

Nehemiah leave to build Jerusalem. 483 years from 445 B.C. reaches 38 A.D. Now, the Lord was crucified in 30 A.D., or, at the latest, 32 A.D. The prophecy therefore overshoots the mark by seven years. It is incorrect to say that "483 years had transpired on the very day that Jesus presented Himself to the nation of Israel as their Messiah and was rejected by them and put to death" (14). No commandment came from the Lord to Artaxerxes. As it came to Gabriel in verse 23, so in verse 25 the reference is to Cyrus, as is well known: "He is my shepherd, and shall perform all my pleasure: even saying to Jerusalem, Thou shalt be built; and to the temple, Thy foundation shall be laid" (Is.44:28; 45:13). "Now in the first year of Cyrus king of Persia, that the word of the Lord by the mouth of Jeremiah might be fulfilled, the Lord stirred up the spirit of Cyrus king of Persia" (Ezra 1:1; Jer.25:12,13). Cyrus loosed the captivity of the people and sent them to rebuild Jerusalem and the temple about 90 years before Nehemiah's mission.

Christ or Antichrist?

A major contention arises about the one who will confirm the covenant for one week in Dan.9:27. Premillennialists see in this, unhesitatingly, a reference to Antichrist who will make a covenant with the Jewish people. He is said to be the prince of verse 26, who will come out of the revived Roman empire of ten nations (15), despite the fact that the empire in the supposed guise of the European Economic Community is already composed of twenty eight nations and will probably increase. Some dispute whether he will be a Jew or a Gentile. Others say that there will be one of each (16). All the Same, he is supposed to defile the rebuilt temple and cause the sacrifice and oblation to cease from it after three and a half years (17). This will be a prelude to the battle of Armageddon, during which Christ will return and gain the ultimate victory. It will be the finest hour of the church since the first century (18). Since the majority of the Jews will be killed in the battle, can anyone still say their end will be glorious? There will be no need for an antichrist to defile the temple. If a temple where sacrifices will be offered is rebuilt, it will be an abomination to the Lord and a defilement. Christ dwells in his temple, the church, by his Spirit (Mt.28:20; 1Cor.6:15,19), yet we are told that God will go back on his tracks to the beggarly elements, which were instituted temporarily, reside in a temple of stone and accept animal sacrifices. Christ's sacrifice is made invalid and the old covenant, "which decayeth and waxeth old" and "is ready to vanish away" (Heb.8:13) will have a new lease of life. The notions of Messianic Judaism of a messiah who will restore the kingdom to Israel have been adopted by Christians.

Dan.9:26 refers to the death of Christ, and to the destruction of the temple and city by the Romans, the people of the coming prince, but not by the prince. The prince's role is mentioned in verse 27. The reason for this is to distinguish between the prince of the people and Messiah the Prince who is the only other person mentioned in the verse. It is not necessary or profitable to investigate every idea of the nature of the covenant and its confirmer. One representative sample is found in Van Kampen's book, The Sign (5). Others could be used to achieve the same purpose. The full text of verse 27 in the book reads: "And he [Antichrist] will make a firm covenant with many [Israel] for one week [seven years], but in the middle of the week he will put a stop to sacrifice and grain offering; and on the wing of abominations will come one who makes desolate [Antichrist, empowered directly by Satan], even until a complete destruction, one that is decreed [at Armageddon], is poured out on the one who makes desolate."

There are serious objections to this statement, and the translation of the Hebrew text is incorrect. To confirm is to verify or make efficacious something which is in existence already. The Hebrew *'vehigbeer'*, *translated "and he shall confirm", means, and he shall establish, strengthen, make firm, make stable, increase or enlarge: a reference to something existent. To make a "firm covenant", as the above translation puts it, implies the formation of a new firm covenant, and this is incorrect. The meaning is to make an existing covenant firm. The role of Antichrist envisaged above is incompatible with the Hebrew text. The obvious reference is to Christ who confirmed by his blood the existing spiritual covenant, the one for all time that God will be the God of his people (Mt.26:28; Mk.14:24; Lk.22:20; 1Cor.11:25; Heb.9:15).* The new covenant is the putting of the law in the heart (Jer.31: 33; Heb.8:6–10) and the taking away of sin. (Ro.11:27). This is the same covenant made with Abraham, but not the "old" temporary covenant which was made in Sinai with the giving of the law. To confirm the covenant with many for one seven indicates that the confirmation was to fall in the last seven when the Lord died and many Jews believed before the major entrance of the Gentiles into the faith. The wrong identification of the covenant confirmer with Antichrist requires the invention of the long gap and the national restoration of Israel. It is said: "But before this last 'week' could take place, Israel needed to gain control of her Promised land (which she did in 1948) and then the entire city of Jerusalem (which she did in 1967)…"(20). The protagonists of this interpretation cannot see how Antichrist can come against Israel if Israel is not there and how the Lord can return before these things have time to happen. If the theory is not true, a whole scheme of interpretation of prophecy will crumble into nothing.

Since the covenant confirmer is the Messiah and not Antichrist, it will be he who, in the midst of the last seven, will cause the sacrifice and oblation to cease, not in a rebuilt temple, but by his death which opened the way to the Holy of Holies (Mt.27:51; Mk.15:38; Lk.23:45) and also made the Holy of Holies, which represented God's residence, redundant. God no longer resided in the Temple. As far as he was concerned, sacrifice and oblation ceased when Christ "appeared to put away sin by the sacrifice of himself" (Heb.9:26; 10:8,9). Jewish sacrifices thereafter were a defiance of God's redemptive work in Christ. The section in Daniel, therefore, does not define Israel's immediate premillennial destiny, but the end of Israel's separation as God's special people and the termination of their special role.

The last part of verse 27 demolishes the Antichrist theory altogether. The literal Hebrew translation is: "And upon wing of abominations a desolator (one making desolate) and until full end and that determined shall pour upon the desolate." The prince of the people was mentioned in verse 26. Since he is not the confirmer of the covenant or the cause of the ceasing of the sacrifice, it would be extremely strange to leave him hanging in the air without a role planned for him. Verse 27 introduces him by the word "and". "And upon wing of abominations a desolator" is the same as: And a desolator upon wing of abominations etc. E.J. Young paraphrased the last statement thus: "And until the full end which has been determined shall fall upon the desolate" (21). The reference is to Titus, the destroyer of the Temple (22). The full end is a tanslation of the Hebrew "*ad-kala*". The meaning is, until the completion, consummation, execution, fulfilling, finishing, perishing, of a thing. It is not the consummation or the end of the age, but the completion of a task. The determined end of utter destruction will fall upon and be completed upon what has been made desolate by the desolator, that is the city and temple. E.J. Young says: "The last half of vs.27 presents one of the principal stumbling-blocks in the way of the dispensational interpretation, and many of the representatives of this school pass over the words in comparative silence" (23). Dan.9:24–27 can be made to include a long gap and an antichrist by speculation only, and not by proper analysis of the passage.

REFERENCES

(1) Hal Lindsey, The Late Great Planet Earth, (Marshall Pickering, Basingstoke, England, 1988), pp. 42–45.

(2) Arthur W. Kac, The Rebirth of the State of Israel, (Marshall Morgan & Scott, London, 1958), p. 25.

(3) Ibid., pp. 364–369.

(4) Ibid., p. 370.

(5) Robert Van Kampen, The Sign, (Crossway Books, Wheaton, Illinois, 1993). pp. 85,86.

(6) Grant R. Jeffrey, Prince of Darkness, (Frontier Research Publications, Toronto, Ontario, 1994), p. 294.

(7) Ibid., pp. 302–312.

(8) Hal Lindsey, ibid., p. 54.

(9) John F. Walvoord, Major Bible Prophecies, (Zondervan Publishing House, Grand Rapids, Michigan, 1991), pp. 171,172.

(10) Robert Van Kampen, ibid., p. 91.

(11) Ibid., pp. 91–95.

(12) John F. Walvoord, ibid., p. 169.

(13) Ibid., pp. 168,169.

(14) Hal Lindsey, There's A New World Coming, (Harvest House Publishers, Eugene, Oregon, 1984), p. 82.

(15) Ibid., p. 85

(16) Grant R. Jeffrey, ibid., p. 34.

(17) Ibid., p. 300.

(18) Marion F. Kremers, God Intervenes in the Middle East, (Companion Press, Shippensburgh, Pennsylvania, 1992), p. 125.

(19) Robert Van Kampen, ibid., pp. 87–95.

(20) Ibid., p. 90.

(21) Edward J. Young, Daniel, (The Geneva Series of Commentaries, The Banner of Truth Trust, Edinburgh, 1988), p. 219.

(22) Ibid., p. 218.
(23) Ibid., p. 219.

RECOMMENDED READING

Edward J. Young, Daniel, (The Geneva Series Commentaries, The Banner of Truth Trust, Edinburgh, 1988).

Chapter Eight
Misguided Eschatology

We live in an age where many look at political and economic events and see in them the signs of the end described in the Bible. Men have done this in the past and were proved wrong. But, it is said, there were essential signs which were missing then and appeared only in our generation, the generation which will witness the battle of Armageddon, the return of Christ and the ushering in of the millennium. Chief among the signs are the rebirth of the state of Israel and the recreation of the new Roman empire risen from the ashes in the shape of the European Community, the beast with ten horns. It does not bother such interpreters that the beast has twenty eight horns already and is growing more horns all the time. They see in Europa riding the bull, which symbol forms part of the European Currency Unit and the stamp of the European Parliament, the woman of the book of Revelation 17 riding the beast. Again, they are not bothered that the beast of Revelation has seven heads and is not a bull. They try to fathom the name of Antichrist, 666 (Rev.13:18), who will come from Europe, or Russia against Israel, but no one ventures to call him Gog since Gog is supposed to be the same person. Should the world last another fifty years there will be people who will say that our generation got it wrong: this or that sign was missing. And so, the matter goes on from generation to generation.

We live in an age of multiplicity: multiplicity of cars in one household, computers, televisions, video recorders, radios and hi-fi sets. The same trend is seen in a multiplicity of resurrections, returns of Christ and Armageddons.

The Return of Christ and Associated Features

It is inconceivable that anyone can deduce from the New Testament the notion of multiple stages for the resurrection (1) and four returns of Christ (2) as he commutes between heaven and earth in the last days. The New Testament is unequivocally clear that there is one event when Christ will return, take the believers to himself, raise the dead, judge the world and bring in the eternal state and that is that.

A woman entered her house and could not locate her disabled aunt immediately. She panicked that her aunt was taken up or raptured by the Lord, while she was left behind. This is one example of those who separate the time of the rapture from the time of the visible return of the Lord on the last day. When the Lord said that two will be in the field, or at the mill and one will be taken, he was speaking of "that day and hour" which is known only to the Father (Mt.24:36–41).

The Lord Jesus said about himself: "for the hour is coming, in the which all that are in the graves shall hear his voice, and shall come forth; they that have done good, unto the resurrection of life; and they that have done evil, unto the resurrection of damnation" (John 5:28–29). This means that there will be one resurrection at the end of time, when all the dead are raised, but there will be two outcomes: either eternal life or damnation. It is incomprehensible how people interpret this verse to mean that there will be two resurrections. The Lord also said of those who believe on him, that he will raise them up on the last day (John 6:38–40,44).

Paul says: "The Lord himself shall descend from heaven with a shout, with the voice of the archangel, and with the trump of God: and the dead in Christ shall rise first: then we which are alive and remain shall be caught up together with them in the clouds, to meet the Lord in the air: and so shall we ever be with the Lord" (1Thess.4:16,17). The voice of the archangel and the *last* trumpet will be on the last day, the day of resurrection. The commotion will indicate that it will be a public and not a secret removal. It will involve, not the living believers only, but their resurrected brothers and sisters who will rise before anyone is taken up. The purpose of being caught up is to meet the returning Lord: like meeting someone at the airport or at the railway station. He comes gloriously to judge the earth, with his saints (1Thess.3:13; Jude 14; Zech.14:5) in the sight of all peoples.

The resurrection, at the sound of the last trumpet, will be of all men, "the just and the unjust" (Jn.5:28,29; Acts 24:15; Dan.12:2). Believers, who will rise on the last day (Jn.6:39,40,44,54), will not be overtaken by the resurrection of unbelievers, for the day of judgment will be of all men (Mt.24:30,31; Acts 17:31), of their secret works (Ro.2:16) and of their every deed (Ro.2:5,6). "Behold, I come quickly; and my reward is with me, to give every man according as his works shall be" (Rev.22:12). It will be a judgment of the quick and the dead (2Tim.4:1), the small and the great (Rev.20:12), the wheat and the tares who will not be separated until then (Mt.13:24–43), the sheep and the goats (Mt.25:31–46), the wicked and the saints (2Thess.1:7–10; Mt.13:49,50; 16:27; Jude 14,15;

2Pet.3:7; 2Tim.4:8; Lk.19:15,26,27; 1Cor.4:5). But it will also be a judgment of the forces of evil, the devil and his fallen angels (2Thess.2:8; Jude 6; 2Pet.2:4; Rev.20:14). All things will be restored to the conditions before the fall of Adam (Acts 3:20,21). There will be new heavens and a new earth (2Pet.3:10–13), and immortality will be the reward of the saints (1Cor.15:42,44,51,52; Phil.3:20,21).

Millennium

In view of the one return, one resurrection, one judgment and the establishment of a new heavens and earth, a millennial reign of Christ on earth becomes an intrusion upon a state which affords no place for it.

The first seven verses of Revelation 20 mention the thousand years six times. Premillennialists believe that Christ will come again and establish a kingdom on earth that will remain for a thousand years. It is very significant that the verses in Revelation never mention the coming of Christ to earth. The verses from 11 to the end of the chapter portray the resurrection of the dead and final judgment, but nowhere is it stated that the Lord will descend on earth to establish a millennial kingdom.

No book in the Bible has been abused as much as the book of Revelation. It is thought by some that the prophets saw real events and translated them into symbols (3). The opposite is true: the prophets saw visions which were symbolic of future events. Daniel saw a ram and a he-goat (Daniel ch.8) and needed the angel's interpretation of what he saw. John, who was acquainted with the visage of the Lord, yet in Revelation chapter one described him as having a sword protruding out of his mouth and eyes as a flame of fire and hair like white wool, because he saw him in that form.

The idea of the millennium comes from Revelation, chapter 20. Verse 4 tells of the *souls* of them that were beheaded for the witness of Jesus who "lived and reigned with Christ a thousand years". The word translated as souls from the Greek also means lives (4). They live and reign with Christ a thousand years. All Christians are alive and reign with Christ. "It is a faithful saying: For if we be dead with him, we shall also live with him: if we suffer, we shall also reign with him" (2Tim.2:11–12.) As we suffer in this life, not in the millennium, we also reign in this life. This is nothing but an assertion of the Christian's union with Christ in his death, resurrection, crucifixion (Ro.6), life and reign.

The first resurrection can be contrasted with the first death, which is a spiritual death, for the first death entered the world through the sin of Adam (Ro.5). It did not cause his immediate physical death. God said to him, "in the day thou eatest thereof thou shall surely die" (Gen.2:17). He died spiritually that day, but his body died nine hundred and thirty years later. We were dead in our sins before we believed and have been resurrected by the Holy Spirit and regenerated. "Buried with him in baptism, wherein also ye are risen with him through the faith of the operation of God, who hath raised him from the dead. And you, being dead in your trespasses and sins…" (Col.2:12–114). Resurrection does not mean going to Heaven when we die, and await the consummation of all things. It means rising from the dead, as we have been spiritually raised from our state of death in sin. As John says in his first epistle, "We know that we have passed from death unto life" and also, "God hath given to us eternal life, and this life is in his Son" (1John3:14; 5:11). The Lord said the same thing before in John 5:24–25: "He that heareth my word, and believeth on him that sent me, hath everlasting **life**, and shall not come into condemnation; **but is passed from death unto life**......**the *dead*** shall hear the voice of the Son of God: and they that hear **shall live**."

The thousand years is a symbolic round figure of long duration describing the gospel age until the Lord's return. It is the age of the first resurrection when those who are dead in sins are raised to new life in Christ. Moreover, the end of Rev. 19 describes that the beast and the false prophet were thrown into the lake of fire. Their destruction is contrasted with the triumph of the saints who live and reign with Christ, not a short period of time when the beast afflicted them, but a long time, a thousand years.

The binding of Satan is definitely figurative, for Satan is a spirit, and how does one bind a spirit with a chain? Remember the words of the Lord Jesus when he said, "how can one enter into a strong man's house, and spoil his goods, except he first bind the strong man? and then he will spoil his goods" (Matt.12:29). The Lord said this in connection with the casting out of devils by the Spirit of God in the previous verse. The devil seems to be rampant and unbound, but let us not forget the presence of the Holy Spirit in the church and the presence of the church in the world. Would not the world be in a more barbaric state if the church never existed and the Holy Spirit did not indwell believers? Being bound does not mean having no influence. We are told in Jude, verse 6, that "the angels which kept not their first estate, but left their own habitation, he hath reserved in everlasting chains under darkness unto the judgment of the great day." The demons possessed and afflicted people when the Lord was on earth, despite them being chained, as the Scripture says. Despite the evil in the world with the agony of war, famine and injustice, the church works for the release of multitudes out of Satan's grip. It heals the wounded and brokenhearted and attends to their needs. In this respect, the world is not in the condition in which it was before the Flood when it deserved utter destruction.

Gog and Armageddon

The Battle of Armageddon is based upon difficult portions of Scripture which some find easy to understand. The argument in its favour is founded primarily upon Ezekiel 38 and 39; Revelation 16 and 17; Isaiah 34; Daniel 11; Joel 3 and Zechariah 14 (5). It is believed that during the last seven year period of Daniel 9, an Arab-African confederacy, a Russian confederacy and a Far Eastern confederacy will attack Israel and will be destroyed by the Lord's appearing. The battle will take place in the plain of Esdraelon, the biblical valley of Jezreel.

Armageddon is synonymous with the Day of the Lord in the Scofield Bible as the title of Isaiah 34 indicates. It also links it with the assault of Gog in Ezekiel 38. Scofield says of Gog: "That the primary reference is to the northern (European) powers, headed by Russia, all agree. The whole passage should be read in connection with Zech.12.1–4; 14. 1–9; Mt.24. 14–30; Rev.14.14–20; 19.17–21. 'Gog' is the prince, 'Magog', his land. The reference to Meshech and Tubal (Moscow and Tobolsk) is a clear mark of identification......The whole prophecy belongs to the yet future 'day of Jehovah' (Isa.2.10–22; Rev.19.11–21), and to the battle of Armageddon (Rev.16.14; 19.19, *note*), but includes also the final revolt of the nations at the close of the kingdom-age (Rev.20.7–9)" (6). He places the battle before the millennium or kingdom-age and at its close. Ellison observed rightly that this is "an illegitimate attempt to have the best of it both ways" (7). Fairbairn noted that Is.34 places the fighting upon the mountains of Edom, Joel 3 in the valley of Jehoshaphat (which is identified traditionally with the valley of Kidron). Zech.14 and Rev.20 place it in the immediate neighbourhood of Jerusalem, while Ezek.38 places it upon the mountains of Israel (8). Armageddon was the valley of Megiddo where Sisera was defeated by Barak and Deborah (Jg.5:19).

Gog – whom premillennialists equate with Antichrist – is mentioned in the Bible in Ezek.38,39 and in Rev.20 only, apart from the personal name of one in the line of Reuben (1Chr.5:4). Premillennialists believe that the battle will take place before the return of Christ. Rev.20 sees Gog making battle against the camp of the saints and the beloved city one thousand years later, after Satan is released. Scofield tried to have it both ways. Others attempt to get out of the difficulty by saying that Gog and Magog of Rev.20 will be descendants of Israel's enemies who will be born during the millennium (9). Using the words of Ellison in another context, it "is an excellent example of the wish being the father of the thought" (10).

Other matters which preclude a literal interpretation have been documented well, such as the seven month period required for the burial of the slain (Ezek.39:12). According to one conservative estimate the dead will total 360 million corpses (11). Apart from this, Gog and his allies will come riding horses and chariots, not tanks, armoured vehicles and supersonic jet fighters. It is said regarding this: "It is interesting to note that the Cossacks have always loved horses and have been recognised as producing the finest army of cavalry in the world. Today they are reported to have several divisions of cavalry. It is believed by some military men that cavalry will actually be used in the invasion of the Middle East just as Ezekiel and other prophets literally predicted" (12). Furthermore, Gog's army will not only use horses in the invasion of Israel, but also ancient instruments of war, such as bows, arrows, swords and spears. Men prefer to accept this incredible notion rather than concede that their interpretation is untenable. It is said: "Preceding the war there will be a genuine disarmament of the world. Under such circumstances, if Russia wanted to attack Israel and lacked modern weapons, she would be able to manufacture quickly and in great quantity weapons that would equip the army in this way" (13). Whoever is inclined to believe this sort of thing is in a hopeless condition to be convinced otherwise. Men claim that Armageddon will be a nuclear battle of unsurpassed magnitude, yet they do not hesitate to state, in the same breath, that this greatest battle of the world will be fought on horseback with bows and arrows!

It was a common thing, that when God comforted his people through the prophets, he judged their sins and judged their enemies before promising temporal blessings followed by eternal blessings through Christ. But the fight with the world and evil, both carnal and spiritual, does not end as if a permanent rest is achievable in this world. The enemies of God's people will rise against them, but God will defend his own. Gog must be placed in this context. The chapters which deal with his assault should not be separated from adjacent chapters and shaped into an isolated prophecy. In Ezek.34, God reprimands the shepherds of Israel who made themselves fat by feeding on the sheep. He will deliver his people and place a faithful shepherd over them, even David, who in his lifetime exerted himself for their good. The reference is, of course, to Christ. God will make a covenant of peace with them and make them dwell safely in their land. Chapter 35 speaks of judgment upon Edom for its affliction of God's people. Chapter 36 adds further comfort to the people and their land. Though they were scattered for their iniquity, God will restore them for his name's sake which has been dishonoured among the heathen. He will take away their stony heart, give them a heart of flesh and put his spirit within them and they will keep his commandments. Chapter 37 gives a graphic picture of the people's restoration and promises their resurrection from their graves and their return to their land from the Babylonian exile. God says again that he will put his spirit within them. He will unite their division, which took place after Solomon's death, and they will no longer worship idols. The restored one nation will have David as an eternal king. The restoration is blended with promises about Christ, being a foretaste of the peace and spiritual prosperity which God's people will experience when He comes as their saviour. After all this comes Gog's invasion and his destruction.

If the contents of the chapters are to be taken literally, then it must be assumed that the people actually possessed hearts of stone, that they will be resurrected from their graves, with David before Antichrist's assault upon Israel. We have not seen the bodies of the Jewish dead rise from their graves when the modern state of Israel – supposed to be a fulfilment of this prophecy – was formed, nor have we seen king David come to life. But, if the prophecy is placed in its legitimate context, then it was fulfilled in part. The people returned to their land, became one nation and did not worship idols any more. They rebuilt the Temple and Jerusalem, but David and the dead were not raised. Fairbairn was right when he wrote: "The prophecy, therefore, has not been accomplished according to the letter in the past; and with so strong and prominent a feature of an ideal sort as the eternal presidency of David, it seems amazing that any one should expect it to be realised after that manner in the ages to come" (14). The promise of a heart of flesh belongs to the spiritual kingdom of Christ, who is David's son. It is given also in Jer.31:33 and was quoted by the writer of the epistle to the Hebrews when he wrote of Christ's eternal priesthood and sacrifice and the benefits arising from it (Heb.8:10; 10:16).

Despite the benefits of Christ to his people, the battle with evil, moral and physical, is not over. They will suffer persecution in the world. The theme of the enemies of Christ and his people rising against them, only to be defeated, is repeated continuously in the book of Revelation. It is the theme of Joel 3 and Zech.14 and the Lord's discourse about the destruction of the Temple and the siege of Jerusalem and the end of the age in Mt.24, Mk.13 and Lk.21. The Lord's coming will be to a world, like in the days of Noah, caring for nothing but its own pleasure, yet busy in its enmity against the people of God. Persecution of believers has been taking place throughout the centuries, but it would appear that when Satan sees that his end is approaching when he is released, he will make one final effort to destroy God's people, knowing that his fate is sealed in the hands of an avenging God. Armageddon is symbolic of this and will be answered by the final day of the Lord, the day of judgment of men and evil spirits. Gog and Magog are the nations to be deceived in the four corners of the world, that is worldwide. Gog in Revelation is a nation and not a prince as in Ezekiel.

When the Bible speaks of the distant future, it does not

name names. Abraham was not told the names of the Pharaohs of oppression, or of the Exodus. Daniel was not told the name of Alexander, but described him in the image of a he-goat. The antichrist is not named, nor the man of sin, nor the false prophet. Even the Messiah was not named Yeshua', meaning Saviour, until the day of his conception. Immanuel represented his role, for it meant, 'Immanu, with us, is El or God, but was not his personal name. Contemporary people or those in the recent past or near future, such as Hazael, Nebuchadnezzar and Cyrus are named. It would be strange to name Gog if he were to come more than 2500 years later. It is necessary to look into the contemporary or recent history of Ezekiel's time in an attempt to find what was represented by Gog.

There was a bodyguard to King Candaules of Lydia in Asia Minor (western modern Turkey), whose name was Gyges. He murdered his master about 685 B.C., usurped his kingdom and ruled for 38 years (15)(16). The Assyrians called him Gugu. The similarity of the name with the Hebrew Gog is obvious. He was at the western fringe of the world in relation to the land of Israel. Gomer, Magog, Meshech and Tubal were sons of Japheth while Togarmah was son of Gomer (Gen.10:2,3). Gomer gave rise to the Gimirrai, of Assyrian records of the seventh century B.C., and the Cimmerians of the Greeks whom Gyges invaded. He met his death while fighting them. Meshech and Tubal are not Moscow and Tobolosk, which were founded in 1147 A.D. and in 1587 A.D. respectively. They were the Mushki of Assyrian records (17) and the Tubali, peoples of Asia Minor located on the south and southeastern coast of the Black Sea at the time of Herodotus. The Mushki lived northeast of Cilicia and the Tubali east of Cappadocia between them and the Euphrates prior to this. The regions are situated now in modern Turkey. The

Mushki invaded the country of the Hittites, including Carchemish and Hamath, about 1200 B.C. (18). Mushki and Tubali were fierce enemies of the Assyrians in the twelfth, eleventh and seventh centuries B.C. Mitas of the Mushki is thought to have been king Midas of the Phrygians of the early eighth century B.C., whose legendary touch turned anything to gold (19). Meshech and Tubal were also the Moschi and Tabereni of Herodotus and formed the nineteenth satrapy of Darius I (548–486) (20). Herodotus lived between 485 and 425 B.C. and therefore wrote of the very recent past. According to Driver the prophecy in Ezek.38 and 39 "is modelled upon the great irruption of the Scythians into Asia (Hdt. I. 104–6), which took place c. 630 B.C." (21)(22). Driver says in the footnote: "Mat is the common Assyrian word for 'land'; and hence 'Magog' has been supposed to be a contraction for *Mat-Gog, 'the land of Gog' (Sayce, Monuments*, 125 f), or (Z. *fur Ass.* 1901, p. 321) for *Mat-Gagaia*, 'the land of Gagaia', a people mentioned in Tell el-Amarna tablets (KB. v. 5) (23). Togarmah is accepted by most commentators to have been the land of Armenia. Ellison says of all this: "When we find that all the names are of tribes on the fringe of the then known world: north, Gog, Magog, Meshesh, Tubal, Gomer, Beth-Togarmah; east, Persia (only just beginning to make its appearance on the Iranian plateau); south, Cush and Put, it becomes intrinsically most probable that we are dealing with a symbolic use, and Rev.20:8 confirms this by calling them 'the nations which are in the four corners of the earth.'" He concludes: "There is no contradiction between 38:4, where God is pictured as drawing Gog to his doom, and Rev.20:8, where Satan is portrayed as the deceiver of the nations. Man must be put to the test, or else it will not be clear what is in him" (24). But the explanation that despite all their blessings, the people of

God and of Christ have to cope with the evil in the world and its enmity until the end, is the most likely explanation of the intrusion of Gog into the picture. This is confirmed in Rev.20 where the struggle of the saints with Satan goes on until the very end of time. The outcome is clear. The victory will belong to Christ and his church at the final consummation of all things. Therefore the idea that Israel must be in their land, otherwise the battle of Armageddon cannot take place, is fanciful speculation.

REFERENCES

(1) Hal Lindsey, There's A New World Coming, (Harvest House Publishers, Eugene, Oregon, 1984), pp. 259,260.

(2) Robert Van Kampen, The Sign, (Crossway Books, Wheaton, Illinois, 1993), pp. 436,437.

(3) Hal Lindsey, ibid., pp. 11,12.

(4) J. Marcellus Kik, An Eschatology of Victory, (Presbyterian and Reformed Theology, 1971), p. 227.

(5) Hal Lindsey, ibid., pp. 209–212.

(6) Scofield Bible, p. 883.

(7) H.L. Ellison, Ezekiel, The Man and his Message, (The Paternoster Press, London, 1956), p. 134.

(8) Patrick Fairbairn, Commentary on Ezekiel, (Kregel Publications, Grand Rapids, Michigan, 1989), p. 431.

(9) Hal Lindsey, ibid., p. 261.

(10) H.L. Ellison, ibid.

(11) Patrick Fairbairn, ibid.

(12) Hal Lindsey, The Late Great Planet Earth, (Marshall Pickering, Basingstoke, 1988), p. 70.

(13) John Walvoord, Major Bible Prophecies, (Zondervan Publishing House, 1991), p. 331.

(14) Patrick Fairbairn, ibid., p. 418.

(15) Herodotus, The Histories, (Penguin Books Ltd., Harmondsworth, Middlesex, 1983), pp. 44,45.

(16) Chambers Biographical Dictionary, (W & R Chambers Ltd., Edinburgh, 1990), p. 644.

(17) John L. McKenzie, Dictionary of the Bible, (Macmillan Publishing Company, New York, 1965), p. 568.

(18) O.R. Gurney, The Hittites, (Penguin Books Ltd., Harmondsworth, Middlesex, 1981), p. 6.

(19) Peter James, Centuries of Darkness, (Jonathan Cape Ltd, London, 1992), pp. 137,138.

(20) Herodotus, ibid., p. 244.

(21) S.R. Driver, The Book of Genesis, (Methuen & Co. Ltd, London, 1913), p. 115.

(22) Herodotus, ibid., pp. 84–85.

(23) S.R. Driver, ibid.

(24) H.L. Ellison, ibid., pp. 134–136.

RECOMMENDED READING

Loraine Boettner, The Millennium, (The Presbyterian and Reformed Publishing Company, Philadelphia, 1958).

Winkie Pratney and Barry Chant, The Return, (Sovereign World, Chichester, 1988).

William Hendriksen, More than Conquerors, (The Tyndale Press, London, 1962).

ESSENTIAL READING

Patrick Fairbairn, The Interpretation of Prophecy, (The Banner of Truth Trust, London, 1964).

J. Marcellus Kik, The Eschatology of Victory.

Chapter Nine
Israel's Restoration

It is unhelpful, when considering a biblical question, to quote verses in favour or against a point of view and leave it at that. It is best to consider principles which govern the issue at hand, in this case, Israel's national restoration.

EVIDENCE FROM THE OLD TESTAMENT

Those who claim that the prophets foretold the national restoration of Israel in the twentieth century must show that the same prophets foretold a further dispersion after the exile and a promise of a return from that dispersion. Promises of a return from Assyria and Babylon should not be used to prove a return in the twentieth century. It would be like the case of a man in our time who discovers a poster offering a reward for the capture of Jesse James, dead or alive, and embarks on an expedition to capture the outlaw.

Israel and the Land

The children of Israel were vital instruments in God's plan of redemption for mankind. God revealed himself to them and through them to the world. This involved giving them laws which governed every detail of their life in its social, economic, national, international and religious aspects. God, moreover, tied all the practices with the land of Canaan. It was his land (Lev.25:23; Dt.32; 43) where he dwelt among his people (Ex.25:8; 29:45,46; Nu.35:34). A statement is repeated frequently, in one form or another, in the last four books of Moses, which says: "When ye come into the land which I give you, then"…you should do this or refrain from doing that (Lev.25:2; Nu.35:10; Dt.6:1; 11:8; 12:1; 18:9 etc.). The covenant, the law and commandments, the feasts and sacrifices, religious and moral matters, all with intricate detail, were laid down to be observed in the land (Dt.11–26). Blessings would follow obedience: the rain would fall, the land would flourish and the people would live in safety. A multitude of curses would follow their departure from the Lord: the land would become barren and they would be scattered in the face of their pursuing enemies (Dt.27–30). The point being made is that the children of Israel could not be separated from their land and continue to observe their religious and social duties. They were tied up to the land with every sinew of their body. Israel in Canaan meant the worship of God in his tabernacle or temple, the Sabbath rest for the people and the land, the year of the Jubilee, the service of the priesthood and many other things. Israel out of Canaan meant the cessation of these practices. Israel in Canaan without the practices would have been an anomaly. Similarly, if the practices were abolished or disregarded and Israel remained in Canaan, it would have been an anomaly. Indeed, when wickedness reigned in the land, the people were driven out of it, not only to the countries of exile, but to neighbouring countries, to Egypt, Ethiopia, North Africa and to more distant places. Is.66:19 mentions a scattering to Tarshish (Spain, or

Sardinia), Pul (Libya), Lud (Lydia), Tubal (in Turkey) and Javan (Greece). That was a more appropriate state of affairs than for Israel to remain in the land and to defile it.

Having said this, it becomes easy to understand why the prophets related the welfare of the land to God's pleasure or anger with his people who understood such an association. When God's wrath is turned, he would gather and restore them to their land and dwell in their midst. He would jealously defend his land against all enemies whom he would punish for working evil against his people and land. This is why prophecies were spoken against Egypt, Damascus, Tyre, Edom, Moab, Philistia, Babylon and other nations who all dealt harshly with Israel. But God's blessings did not stop with the land. He looked into the future and promised better days and endless blessings through his anointed one, the servant, the branch, who would bring in everlasting righteousness. Such promises were often made in terms of the people's deliverance from their enemies and their settlement peacefully in their land. It was a constant practice of the prophets to do so. Apart from the immediate return from Assyria and Babylon and wherever they were scattered, and apart from such gathering being employed as a pattern for the ingathering in Christ, there is nothing said about a future dispersion and regathering. Everything ends with the Messiah.

Prophetic Imagery

It is not an exaggeration to say that the people, their obligations and their land formed one issue. It was natural that the prophets, when speaking of future blessings in Christ, should use contemporary language and employ images from the past and present to which the people could relate. Indeed, the prophets made a habit of speaking in this manner. Isaiah, in chapter 11, speaks of the days of the branch and root of Jesse, that is Christ, who will be a standard to the heathen and the remnant of Israel. He tells of the healing of the rift between the northern and southern kingdoms of Israel and Judah, the gathering of God's people from the corners of the earth and their triumph over their enemies who will serve them. He also uses such images as the destruction of the tongue of the Red Sea, which in the time of the Exodus formed a barrier to their escape from the pursuing armies of Pharaoh. The Euphrates will not hinder their return from the land of Assyria and will be divided into seven streams. These images told of their return from exile, the second time (v.11), the first time being from Egypt, not as some presume, a second exile in the future. Similar images are used in Zech.10:10,11 where God shows his intention to complete the return and bring back his people from Egypt and Assyria by smiting the waves in the sea and drying the deeps of the river. These images went beyond a physical restoration from exile. They were used to proclaim the day of the root of Jesse, who will not only gather the remnant of God's people, but will also draw the Gentiles into a living relationship with God. The physical restoration represented the spiritual restoration in Christ's kingdom with its solidarity, safety and peace. If, as some believe, the prophecies refer to our day, then they have not been fulfilled literally, nor can they be. The Philistines and Moabites and Ammonites no longer exist as peoples and their presence is essential for a literal fulfilment. The "tongue of the Egyptian sea" was not destroyed, but was opened by man into the Mediterranean through the Suez Canal. The Euphrates did not become seven streams, nor is there need for such geological manifestations. The Jews came to Palestine from Africa and the Middle East by modern means of transport and traversed the Euphrates along its bridges. They did not have to walk over dryshod.

It should be remembered that most of the prophets prophesied before or during the Assyrian and Babylonian captivities. The context must not be ignored, nor should passages which mention Assyria, Babylon and the Medes be taken to indicate a restoration in our day. Isaiah 13 speaks of the day of the Lord in his vengeance against Babylon. Therefore the return of chapter 14 is from Babylon following its destruction by the Medes, not from present day Iraq. The same can be said of Is.43 where God will redeem his people and punish Babylon. Passages found in Is.49 onwards have to do with the kingdom of Christ, the servant of the Lord, and are spoken of in terms of restoration and redemption. Isaiah 49 provides a notable example. The physical regathering forms only a part of the fulfilment of the ingathering in Christ, who will raise up Jacob and restore the preserved of Israel and be given a light to the Gentiles that salvation may be to the ends of the earth. In this Messianic context, men will crowd into the church and it would appear that there will not be enough room for them. It is most unnatural to imagine, when the passage speaks clearly of Christ's work and its benefits, that it reverts suddenly to the physical aspect of Jerusalem and the Jewish people. To introduce a physical restoration at this point would do violence to the topic of redemption which engaged the prophet.

The Post-Exilic Prophets

The post-exilic prophets were Haggai, Zechariah and Malachi. The timing of Joel's prophecy is disputed. It should be expected that these foretold a dispersion after the rejection of the Messiah and a regathering later. Haggai prophesied in the second year of Darius (420 B.C.) and Zechariah in the second and fourth years. There were still Jews in Assyria and Babylonia who had not returned. Haggai reproved the people for their neglect in building the Temple and encouraged Zerubabel, the governor of Judah, and Joshua, the high priest, to go about the task. The building was frustrated until the second year of Darius when it was carried out through the instigation of Haggai and Zechariah. It was completed in the sixth year of Darius (Ezra 4:5,24; 5:1; 6:14,15). Malachi reprimanded the people for their profanity and neglect of the covenant. Neither he nor Haggai said anything about their dispersion and restoration. Zechariah's prophecy is taken by many to refer to the regathering in our time and the final assault of the nations upon Jerusalem before the return of Christ.

Zechariah looked beyond the restoration of the people who still lived "with the daughter of Babylon" (2:7). His eye was upon the non-Jewish nations who shall "be joined to the Lord", to whom God "shall speak peace" (2:11; 9:10). This is why Jerusalem will have a multitude within it and could not be measured, for the Lord will be her wall and Christ's dominion will be "from sea even to sea, and from the river even to the ends of the earth" (2:1–5; 9:10). The extent of his dominion is reminiscent of the borders of the land of Canaan, except its limit is not from the river (Euphrates) to the river of Egypt, but to the ends of the earth. A spiritual truth is pictured in the form of a physical image. The Lord had returned to Zion and will dwell in the midst of Jerusalem (8:3). The same can be said of the blessings which would follow the coming of Christ, the Lord's servant, the branch, the king of Zion. Men are pictured sitting under their vines and fig trees, an image of peace and tranquillity (3:8–10). Other images are the cutting off of the chariot, the war horse and the bow from Ephraim and Jerusalem, the deliverance of the prisoners "out of the pit wherein is no water": a reminder of the pit into which Joseph was placed by his brethren (9:10,11). The restoration of chapter eight was coupled with the conversion of the nations, where men are pictured as taking hold of the skirt of a Jew so that they can seek the Lord (8:23).

Zechariah 11 puts the prophet in the place of a shepherd who represents Christ, the true shepherd who was rejected. God's covenant of protection of his people from the Gentiles was removed, symbolised by the breaking of the staff Beauty. They would fall prey to their enemies. When the prophet was given the hire of a manservant gored by an ox, namely thirty pieces of silver (Ex.21:32), the staff called Bands was broken to symbolise a dissension among the Jewish people. It would appear that all is lost, that there is no hope for God's people who will be fodder for their masters. Amidst the gloom comes chapter 12, which speaks of Jerusalem being a trembling to the nations who come against her. God will save the tents of Judah "in that day" and will pour upon the house of David and the inhabitants of Jerusalem the spirit of grace and supplication and they shall mourn for him whom they pierced, each family apart. Here again, in an image of God's deliverance is a promise of blessings in Christ. The first fulfilment took place on the day of Pentecost when the Jews gathered at Jerusalem cried out: "Men and brethren, what shall we do?" (Acts 2:37). A further fulfilment has been taking place for centuries and, by God's grace, will continue until the Jewish people are grafted again into the olive tree from which they were broken (Ro.11).

A parallel passage in the New Testament regards the

deliverance in Christ as being a deliverance from the people's enemies. When Zacharias, John's father, was filled with the Holy Ghost, he said that God "hath raised up a horn of salvation for us in the house of his servant David…that we should be saved from our enemies, and from the hand of all that hate us…that we being delivered out of the hand of our enemies might serve him without fear" (Lk.1:67–79). The Holy Spirit, who spoke through the prophets, spoke through Zacharias and proclaimed the redemption which Christ would bring, in Old Testament terms of deliverance from the enemy. This deliverance was not fulfilled literally and untold misery and enmity followed the Jewish people after the majority rejected Christ (see chapter one).

If Zech.12 is taken to indicate a future siege of Jerusalem when Christ will return and the Jews will be converted, then a genealogical difficulty arises. The house of David and of Nathan his son (2Sam.5:14) and the house of Levi and of Shimei his son (Nu.3:18) will mourn apart (vv.12,13). Who can trace his genealogy thus far? Levy and Cohen may come from the house of Levi, but what of Shimei, David and Nathan? The Jewish dispersion ensured that no one is able to trace his genealogy to Nathan and Shimei. The last accurate genealogy belongs to Christ as recorded in the gospels.

Zechariah 13 continues the narrative of "in that day" when a fountain shall be opened for sin and uncleanness and when Christ the shepherd will be smitten and the sheep will be scattered. This shows that the reference all along has been to the redemption in our Lord's sacrifice and not to the seven year period before the Lord's return. "And it shall come to pass, that in all the land, saith the Lord, two parts therein shall be cut off and die, but the third shall be left" and refined as silver and gold and "I will say, It is my people: and they shall say, The Lord is my God" (vv.7–9). The picture is of one third believing on Christ against two thirds rejecting him, that is the smaller number of the whole will believe, not a literal third. Then comes chapter 14 with the day of the Lord, not unexpectedly. When Ezekiel prophesied of the restoration of Israel and of Christ's kingdom in chapter 37, he brought in the assault of Gog and his host. When Joel prophesied of the outpouring of the Holy Spirit in chapter two, he then spoke of the nations coming against his people and their judgment. Zechariah does the same thing. He gathers the nations against Jerusalem and speaks of their judgment on the day of the Lord. The comments which were made regarding Gog's assault apply to Zechariah's prophecy. The church will continue to contend with evil and persecution, but God is on her side. The remnant of the nations will believe and will come to Jerusalem to observe the feast of tabernacles, that is they will remember God's deliverance and offer the sacrifices of praise. There will be a final day of the Lord when Satan and all God's enemies will be destroyed. The chapter describes in figurative terms the state of affairs which will culminate in the return of Christ. It cannot be said to describe what will happen literally. The feast of tabernacles involves burnt offerings and sacrifices (Lev.23:33–43), as is indeed mentioned in the last verse of Zechariah. It is far-fetched to imagine that Christ's return will be followed by a millennial kingdom in which there will be a return to the old Jewish system of sacrifices which were images of Christ's sacrifice.

EVIDENCE FROM THE NEW TESTAMENT

It should be accepted by Christians that the Lord's

interpretation and that of his apostles of Old Testament truths should form the basis of interpretation by all believers. The restoration of Israel in the Old Testament included the physical and the spiritual: the former often represented the latter. Since a national restoration formed a recurring theme in the Old Testament, it should be expected that it would have taken a prominent place in the New Testament. Instead of a restoration, the Lord foretold the destruction of the temple and of Jerusalem. He did not proceed to foretell the restoration of things to their former state.

The Lord did not condone or encourage the Jewish nationalistic aspirations of his day. Although he preached repentance, faith and the kingdom of God to the house of Israel to whom he came, his mission went beyond them. God's worship was no longer the property of certain people in mount Gerizim or in Jerusalem, but belonged to all who "worship the Father in spirit and in truth" (Jn.4:20–24) for Christ came to die for the sins of the whole world.

The organic unity of the kingdom of God was taught by the Lord in his parables. He was the basis of this unity. The kingdom was the living mustard seed which grew into a bush, the leaven which leavened the lump, the vine and its branches and the shepherd and his flock. He taught that the visible organisation of God's people contained the true members of the kingdoms and others who did not belong to it. This came in the parables of the sower, the wheat and the tares, the net cast into the sea, the evil husbandmen who killed the servants and the son of their master. His brethren were no longer those according to the flesh, not even his mother and brothers by virtue of their natural kinship, but all who did the Father's will. The kingdom of God included the centurion whose servant was sick, the Syrophoenician woman whose daughter was possessed by a devil and the many who will come from the east and west and sit with Abraham and Isaac and Jacob. But unbelievers of the natural seed will be cast into outer darkness (Mt.8:12), being of their father the devil (Jn.8:44). Their privilege of race was lost. The kingdom was to be taken from them and given to a nation bringing its fruits (Mt.21:43). The sum of the matter is that the Lord was concerned with the spiritual and not the national aspects of his brethren according to the flesh.

Some find in certain sayings of the Lord a reference to the national restoration of Israel. When the Lord lamented over Jerusalem he said: "Behold your house is left unto you desolate. For I say unto you, Ye shall not see me henceforth, till ye shall say, Blessed is he that cometh in the name of the Lord" (Mt.23:38,39; Lk.13:35). The first statement concerned the coming desolation of Jerusalem; the second probably of the time of his return. The second statement does not specify the nature of events at that time, nor can it mean that Jerusalem will be inhabited by a sovereign Jewish nation practising its ancient religion. Jerusalem was under Roman domination, yet the Lord addressed it in terms of its Jewish inhabitants. There will be no second chance for anyone on the day of judgment when he returns. The people had said already, "Blessed is he that cometh in the name of the Lord" (Mt.21:9; Mk.11:9) and "blessed is the King of Israel" and "blessed be the kingdom of our father David that cometh in the name of the Lord" (Jn.12:13; Mk.11:10; Lk.19:38), but the following week they cried out, "Away with him, crucify him" (Jn.19:6,15; Mk.15:13,14; Mt.27:22,23; Lk.23:21).

Another saying of the Lord: "And Jerusalem shall be trodden down of the Gentiles, until the times of the Gentiles be fulfilled" (Lk.21:24), is seen by many to have been fulfilled in 1967 when Jerusalem came under Israeli domination. The statement does not determine the nature of the times of the Gentiles. It could mean until the gospel is published among all nations (Mk.13:10), or when the redemption of the elect from the Gentiles has been accomplished (Ro.11:25). The meaning would be quaint if it signified that Jerusalem shall be ruled by the Gentiles until it is no longer ruled by them. Nothing is said of Jerusalem's condition thereafter, or of a national restoration. It is nearly fifty years since 1967, but the world still plods on as a weary man.

As with the Lord, so it was with his disciples. Whereas before the day of Pentecost they were confused about the whole issue of Israel's kingdom (Acts 1:6), they were completely silent about the subject thereafter. The Lord answered them with the church in his mind. It was for this reason that he asked them to wait in Jerusalem until they were filled with the Holy Spirit and with power. The contrast between their question then and their subsequent preaching is remarkable. The Pharisees also thought that God's kingdom was physical, having expected its sudden appearance (Lk.19:11), as did the people who sang Christ's praises on Palm Sunday. But it was a kingdom among them which does not come by observation or external show (Lk.17:20). They considered the physical; the Lord considered the spiritual.

When Peter was filled with the Holy Spirit, his understanding changed from the natural to the spiritual in a most profound manner. He spoke of Christ, enthroned on David's throne, as the one who fulfilled God's covenant with Abraham (Acts 2:30–36; 3:25,26). Old Testament terms and concepts, such as inheritance, priesthood and temple, chosen people, holy nation and the sheep of God, were applied to all believers, not to natural Israel

(1Pet.1:4; 2:5,9). He wrote of the day of the Lord which will usher a new heavens and a new earth (2Pet.3:10–13). Nowhere did he speak or write of Israel's national restoration to its former state with its temple worship.

Paul, also, used terms in his theology which belonged to ancient Israel. God's temple was no longer a building of stone, but the believers' body (1Cor.6:19). Believers are the Israel of God (Ro.9:6–8; Gal.6:16), the real children of Abraham, the true circumcision, the heirs of the kingdom of God and of Christ (Gal.3:7,29; 4:28; Phil.3:3; Ro.2:29; Acts 20:32; Eph.1:11,14; 5:5; Col.3:24; Gal.5:21). The Gentiles, who were strangers from the covenants of promise and the commonwealth of Israel, have become fellow citizens with the saints and of the household of God in the holy temple of the Lord (Eph.2:11–22; Gal.3:28). The writer of the epistle to the Hebrews, also, said that believers were heirs of the Old Testament promises, not of earthly things, but of eternal blessings in Christ (Heb.6:12; 9:15). They have come to Mount Sion and the heavenly Jerusalem (Heb.12:22), which have taken the place of earthly Jerusalem in the annals of God. The epistles of John, James and Jude said nothing of Israel's restoration. This leaves Paul's discourse in Ro.9–11.

Paul shows in Romans 9 that not all Abraham's natural seed are the children of promise. God elected to have mercy on whom he willed from Jews and Gentiles alike. Of Israel, he chose a remnant unto salvation. Chapter 10 shows how this worked out: Israel misunderstood the purpose of the law and sought righteousness through that instrument and not by faith in Christ. Paul says then: "Hath God cast away his people? God forbid. For I also am an Israelite, of the seed of Abraham, of the tribe of Benjamin. God hath not cast away his people which he foreknew" (Ro. 11:1,2). This meant that God has not rejected his ancient people from redemption in Christ, for he himself was one of them, a proof of God's faithfulness. A remnant was chosen from them, but the majority were hardened. This proved of inestimable benefit to the Gentiles who received the gospel through Israel's fall. If their fall was a blessing, the benefits of their reconciliation will be as life from the dead.

God preserved the Jews for their ultimate redemption, not for the restoration of their earthly inheritance. It is inconceivable that God should bless the nations through Christ without blessing the natural seed through whom Christ came. They have been in spiritual bondage and exile, in spiritual Egypt and Babylon, apart from a remnant in every generation. The time will come when the prodigal son will return to his father's arms. This is their glorious prospect, not their imagined slaughter in the battle of Armageddon. There has been one olive tree of God's people from the beginning. Israel formed the natural branches, some of which were cut off because of unbelief, while believing Gentiles were grafted in. The tree will not be complete without Israel, "for the gifts and calling of God are without repentance." As the Gentiles obtained mercy through Israel's unbelief, so will Israel obtain mercy through the effort of the Gentiles to bring them to Christ. Paul uses Isaiah's words to make his own prophecy. Isaiah said: "And the Redeemer shall come *to Zion, and unto them that turn from transgression in Jacob" (Is.59:20). This was fulfilled by the coming of Christ and the redemption of the Jews who believed on him. But now,* "there shall *come out* of Sion the Deliverer, and shall turn ungodliness from Jacob" (Ro.11:26). The Deliverer shall come out of and not to Zion, that is, out of the church through whose preaching Israel will obtain mercy (1). Whereas it has been their minority who believed during the past twenty centuries, the majority will turn to Christ in time. But, unfortunately it has been too late for the multitude who died in unbelief.

Paul's discussion concerns the spiritual salvation of the Jews and has nothing to do with their national restoration. Their conversion may be gradual and the restoration of their ancient land is not a necessity for this. If the remnant of the Gentiles were to benefit from Israel's conversion, it would be more appropriate if Israel lived among them.

Spiritual Israel has replaced natural Israel in God's plan. Israel's election and temporal blessings were a historical parable to all believers. God's ancient people have not been discarded by him. They entered his kingdom in small numbers in the past and are entering now in greater numbers. Christians must seek the salvation of the Jews worldwide.

REFERENCE

(1) Patrick Fairbairn, The Interpretation of Prophecy, (The Banner of Truth Trust, London, 1964), pp. 283–285.

Chapter Ten
Why Did God Choose a
People and a Land?

The following argument deals with the basic reason as to why God chose Abraham and his seed. This question should have been asked by Christian Zionists long before they started misappropriating the Scriptures to their own ends.

Why did God Choose Abraham and his Seed?

There are several answers to the question, but one ultimate reason for God's election of Abraham and his descendants from Isaac and Jacob. The first reason was that God loved them. "The Lord did not set his love upon you, nor choose you, because ye were more in number than any people...but because the Lord loved you." "The Lord had a delight in thy fathers to love them, and he chose their seed after them" (Dt.7:7,8; 10:15; 4:37). "Was not Esau Jacob's brother? saith the Lord: yet I loved Jacob" (Mal.1:2).

The second reason was restricted to the punishment of the Amorites (Gen.15:16). The heathen nations worshipped idols with immorality. But their cup of iniquity was full when they began to sacrifice their children to their gods. "Every abomination to the Lord, which he hateth, have they done unto their gods; for even their sons and their daughters have they burnt in the fire to their gods" (Dt.12:31). God intended their destruction when they plumbed the depths of wickedness (Dt.18:12). He warned his people not to follow their example (Lev.18:21; 20:2–5), but some did (2Ki.16:3; 21:2,6; 2Chr.33:6; Jer.7:31; 19:5; Ezek.20:26).

The third reason was that God used them as a means of his special revelation to mankind and its preservation in the Scriptures. After the days of Noah, mankind degraded itself in iniquity and lost the knowledge of God. Although civilisation flourished in ancient Iraq and Egypt, it was the civilisation of gods and goddesses and their offspring. The epics of Gilgamesh and the Creation tell how man sought after immorality, though vainly and how he was created to be slave to gods who disagreed about his fate before they brought the flood upon him. Abraham knew God but his father and kindred continued in their paganism. The children of Israel were an island of people, ruled by the living God in the midst of a heathen world. It was important that they should be separated in a land and that righteousness be the pattern of their lives. There is no need to elaborate upon God's revelation of his compassion, justice and holiness. His character is summed up by the words: "Ye shall be holy: for I the Lord your God am holy" (Lev.19:2; 11:44; 20:7,26). God showed them in his law, which was too severe to keep (Acts 15:10), the necessity of grace and salvation in Christ. The law was "our schoolmaster to bring us to Christ" (Gal.3:24). Christ's atonement was typified by the blood sacrifices of Leviticus 1–8, the scapegoat of chapter 17 and by the sacrifices of the Passover and the Day of Atonement.

Apart from the law being the instrument by which we may know our need of the saviour, the whole history of the children of Israel was a living parable, especially to those who believe. Their enslavement in Egypt showed God's deliverance from bondage into the liberty of the promised land. "Now these things were our examples, to the intent we should not lust after evil things, as they also lusted. Neither be idolaters as were some of them... Neither let us commit fornication...Neither let us tempt Christ...Neither murmur. Now all these things happened unto them for ensamples: and they are written for our admonition" (1Cor.10:6–11). God slew the rebellious generation in the wilderness lest they enter the land (Heb.3–4). "Let us labour therefore to enter into that rest, lest any man fall after the same example of unbelief" (Heb.4:11).

The fourth and ultimate reason why God chose Abraham and his seed was to ensure the incarnation of his Son, the Lord Jesus Christ. The transcendent reason for Abram's call was: "And in thee shall all the families of the earth be blessed" (Gen.12:1–3). The promise towered above all national boundaries and was not limited to any era of time. It was made before the promise of the land was given. The promise of the land was secondary and subservient to the blessing of mankind. The making of Abram into a great nation was also to serve the same purpose. When God told Abraham of the imminent destruction of the cities of the plain, it was because he "shall surely become a great and mighty nation, and all the nations of the earth shall be blessed in him" (Gen.18;18). In other words, had God not intended to make Abraham the channel of blessing, he would not have made him a great and mighty nation, nor given him the land. The promise was confirmed to Abraham when he was willing to sacrifice his son (Gen.22:17,18). Could it have been otherwise when God intended to offer his own Son for the sins of the world? Similarly, when the promise was confirmed to Isaac and Jacob (Gen.26:3,4; 28:13,14), it was tied up with the blessing of mankind. The land was not to be given for its own sake, nor were Abraham, Isaac and Jacob to become as the stars of heaven for multitude for their own sakes. The reason which occasioned these secondary promises had to do with the advent of the saviour. This was the only part of the covenant which was mentioned by Peter in his sermon to the Jews when he saw its fulfilment in the Lord Jesus Christ (Acts 3:25), because it was the ultimate aim of the covenant. Paul does not leave any possibility for misunderstanding that Christ was the means of the blessing: "Now to Abraham and his seed were the promises made. He saith not, And to seeds, as of many; but as of one, And to thy seed, which is Christ." Those in Christ are heirs to the spiritual promises and are the spiritual seed of Abraham (Gal.3:16,29). The aim of God's covenant with the patriarchs was spiritual. It national aspect was never intended to be of supreme significance, but was the instrument by which the spiritual aim was fulfilled.

God promised a saviour, the seed of the woman, in the garden of Eden (Gen.3:15). He had to be a man: "For verily he took not on him the nature of angels; but he took on him the seed of Abraham" (Heb.2:16). How could the Saviour come and his coming be known? What guarantee was there that he would not be lost amidst the confusion of the rebellious human race? What if he came to China, India or Egypt? Would any, in a world that did not know God, listen to a miracle worker who claimed to be the Son of God who came to give his life a ransom for sinners? Would he not have been regarded as a novelty in a culture knowing only wizardly deceptions and witchcraft? It becomes obvious that God needed a special people in a specified land who were trained to accept miracles and expect a promised Messiah. The nation had to be made ready for the coming ruler from the tribe of Judah (Gen.49:10), the great Prophet of Dt.18:15, the king who would sit on David's throne (Is.9:7; Ps.132:11; Lk.1:32,69; Jer.23:5) and the servant of the Lord who would give his life a ransom for many (Is.53). The town of his birth was specified (Mic.5:2; Mt.2:6). It was no wonder therefore that when John came baptising the Jews wondered whether he was the Christ (Jn.1:20; 3:28). Even the woman of Samaria expected the coming of the Messiah (Jn.4:25). Mary, the mother of Jesus, recognised the significance of his birth and praised God who "hath holpen his servant Israel, in remembrance of his mercy; as he spoke to our forefathers, to Abraham, and to his seed for ever" (Lk.1:54,55). It was revealed to Simeon "by the Holy Ghost, that he should not see death before he had seen the Lord's Christ". He understood the significance of God's covenant with Abraham as being the means of God's redemption: "a light to lighten the Gentiles, and the glory of thy people Israel" (Lk.2:25–32). The light of the Gentiles was Abraham's seed through whom all the families of the earth will be blessed. The glory of Israel was their saviour. The gospel was first preached to Israel then to the world. Christ was the culmination of Israel's hopes, the fulfilment of God's promises, the expectation of Anna who looked for redemption in Israel (Lk.2:36–38). If God had not prepared the people for this great event, nothing would have been known of him. They were returned from the Assyrian and Babylonian exiles to await his coming. Although his own rejected him, the New Testament church was first composed of Jews who believed before the road was opened wide for the Gentiles.

Eusebius names the first fifteen bishops of Jerusalem until 135 A.D. and says that all were of the Circumcision (1).

When the four reasons which have been discussed are taken in turn, it becomes obvious that God fulfilled his purposes in the election of Abraham and his seed. He loved his ancient people, loves them still and seeks their salvation in Christ. The Amorites are no longer in existence and their punishment was meted out. God's revelation to man has been preserved in the Scriptures. The Lord Jesus Christ came and accomplished his vicarious atonement. The gospel is being preached to all nations, to the Jews and the Gentiles. There is therefore no further role for the Jewish people and the land of Israel in a physical sense.

Why did God Choose the Land of Canaan?

Civilisation started in ancient Iraq two thousand years before it began in Greece. Kingdoms and empires rose and fell before the inhabitants of Europe emerged from barbarism. It was not in ancient Iraq, but in the land of Canaan, that God decided to work out his plan for mankind. It is interesting that he chose a family from ancient Iraq through whom he would show his mighty deeds. Iraq lies between two rivers and the land is fertile. The promised land was described as a land of milk and honey. Its region in Lebanon would have been watered by the Hasbani, Litani and al-'Asi rivers. Although the Jordan valley is well irrigated, the Palestinian part of the land depended upon rainfall for its cultivation. It was the region in which the children of Israel lived to a large extent. The land experienced famines in the days of the patriarchs. It was during a famine that Jacob moved into Egypt, a rich land fed by the Nile. The river did not prevent famine when the conditions were present, but Egypt was less likely to know famine than the land of Canaan. The delta of the Nile is one of the richest lands on earth. As far as Canaan was concerned, its dependence on rainfall was paramount. God, who controlled the rain, sent it in blessing and withheld it in chastisement. Canaan was ideal for the sequestration of his people under his government. Had Egypt, or Iraq, been the land of promise and God dried up the rivers, other peoples in Africa, or in Turkey and Syria, would have suffered as a result of his people's iniquity. We only need to remember their apostasy in Elijah's day and the drought which ensued to understand how God was able to punish them without involving other nations. God was teaching them all the time to depend upon him alone.

Another significance of the land of Canaan was its people, composed of different tribes with their cities and chieftains. It was also surrounded by enemies on all sides, except for the sea. This, combined with the hilly and mountainous nature of much of the land, made the rebellion of local groups easy. God would raise his people's neighbouring enemies against them in times of disobedience and would save them and give them rest when they repented. He used this means to urge his people to put their trust in him at all times.

A further reason for God's choice of Canaan was its situation as a land bridge between Africa and Asia. It could be overrun easily by Egyptians, Babylonians, Assyrians, Chaldeans, Persians and Greeks. Such nations were empire builders and each dominated Canaan at one time or another. Its defence depended upon God and his people's loyalty to him. He could give sway to their enemies, or destroy Sennacherib's army. The people's life was a constant test of their faithfulness to God. Canaan was therefore the ideal country where God would encourage his people to trust him continuously, the Lord of hosts, mighty in battle.

Conclusion

Those who regard the future physical role of the Jewish people to be of primary importance in God's plan behave as though the history of redemption started with the election of Abraham. They confuse the aim with the means and set forth the means to be the end to which all things must proceed. It is like a man who sees a fine painting and begins to contemplate in his mind the wonderful materials which were used in its creation. Or, one is shown a magnificent building and remarks that the scaffolding erected during its construction must have been great. His admiration for a painting or an edifice does not go beyond the tools which were used in its production. Such is the case with those who do not realise that the children of Israel were the instrument of God in his plan to redeem men and women from every nation through Christ. The redemption of the Gentiles was not an afterthought, but the primary reason for God's election of Israel, the election which ensured the incarnation of the Son. The role of Israel as a separate people was temporary from the start until the Saviour came and all that was to be accomplished was accomplished. The artificial wall of partition which God built during the season of Israel's sequestration was demolished after the Lord Jesus Christ came. God was faithful: the seed of the woman did bruise the serpent's head. It is a terrible thing to be short-sighted, unable to stand back and see the great panorama of salvation.

It is foolish to concentrate upon chisels and brushes rather than upon the finished work of the artist. To magnify the Jewish people above their state is only a trifle short of idolatry.

REFERENCE

(1)   Eusebius, The History of the Church, (Penguin Books Ltd, Harmondsworth, Middlesex, 1983), p. 156.

Chapter Eleven
An Everlasting Possession

One final problem remains, which is rarely discussed, if ever, by those who agree that Israel's restoration is spiritual and not physical. It is the part of the promise to Abram which says: "For all the land which thou seest, to thee will I give it, and to thy seed *for ever, "for an everlasting possession"* (Gen.13:15; 17:8).

The first thing that must be considered is the relationship of the promise to its historical fulfilment. Abraham was a stranger in the land until the end, "for he looked for a city which hath foundations, whose builder and maker is God" (Heb.11:8–10). He understood the spiritual meaning of the covenant of God with him. When the Lord brought the children of Israel out of Egypt, he destroyed that generation because of their unbelief. The unrighteous shall have no part in the Lord's inheritance. Vacillating between faith in God and idolatry, the children of Israel had a hard time possessing the land, but succeeded in the days of David and Solomon. They began to lose it, thereafter, piecemeal until the divided kingdoms were led into captivity. The land's possession was conditional upon obedience to God, not as modern Christian Zionists say that God was to bring them back in the twentieth century in unbelief. After their return to the land from the Assyrian and Babylonian exiles, the people were largely subject to other nations. They were scattered for nearly two thousand years after the destruction of the Temple in 70 A.D. It cannot therefore be said that the land was their everlasting possession. They possessed it for a far lesser period than they were dispossessed of it. The answer to this discrepancy lies in the fact that possession was conditional upon obedience. It is incredible to conclude from this that since actual possession was temporary, the promise must be fulfilled in the millennium.

There are three legitimate possibilities for the meaning of "everlasting" and "for ever". One meaning refers to eternity, another, to the end of time and a third, to the end of an assigned period.

Future eternity can be dismissed as being the intended meaning. The earth will be destroyed and there will be a new heavens and a new earth (2Pet.3:10–13). A millennial possession is not eternal.

Equating the meaning of "for ever" with the end of time is not tenable. It neglects the true aim of the covenant, namely, the blessing of mankind through Christ. Vital religious practices were decreed in the Old Testament "for ever", although they were of a temporary nature, awaiting their fulfilment in Christ. The feasts of the passover, atonement and tabernacles; feasts of expiation and various offerings, such as the meat, heave and the offerings of the consecration of the priests, were all prescribed for ever. Other practices involved the tabernacle with its continually burning oil lamps, although the tabernacle was temporary and was replaced by the Temple. The portion of the priests from the heave offering, the washing of their hands, the wearing of the mitre and its plate and many other things were to be observed for ever (Ex.12:24; Lev.23:14,21, 31,41; 16:29;

6:18; 7:34,36; 10:15; Nu.18:8,11,23; Ex.27:21; 28:43; Lev.24:3, etc.). It should not be disputed that ordinances ordained for ever were abolished by Christ's atonement. The Aaronic priesthood with all its ceremonial and ritual regulations, its washing and garments, was replaced by the priesthood of believers, although it was established as an everlasting priesthood (Ex.40:15). Practices which belonged to the covenant at Horeb were to be observed continually by the children of Israel "throughout their generations", yet they were abolished (Heb.8–9). The only thing that remains is the new covenant, the gospel and the sacraments of the Lord's supper and baptism. Those who anticipate a return to the old things demolish the work of the Redeemer.

There were other practices instituted for ever which were obviously of a temporary nature. The use of silver trumpets "for the calling of the assembly, and for the journeying of the camps" (Nu.10:2,8), was a statute for ever. It should not have been expected that the children of Israel would be wandering in the desert until the end of time. Another example concerned the slave with an opportunity to be set free, but chose to remain in his master's house. The piercing of his ear confirmed him a slave for ever (Dt:15:17), although his life was transient. It must be concluded that "for ever" does not necessarily mean until the end of time.

Before the third meaning of "for ever" is discussed, it is useful to consider the Hebrew words which the Bible uses in all instances. They are *'ad 'olam* and *'olam*, the *'a* and *'o* being the guttural letter ayin. *'Ad* by itself means immortality, or ever, never-ending, but it also bears the meaning of until, for the purpose of, during, while, unto, as far as. *'Olam* means for ever, everlasting, eternity, always, but it also means the distant future, ages, long duration, world, pleasures of life, universe, encompassing, environment, emptiness and humanity. The two words together, *'ad 'olam*, mean for ever, continual, always.

The promise to Abram in Gen.13:15 employs the words *'ad 'olam*, while in that in 17:8, the word is *'olam*, translated into "everlasting". The "everlasting" of the English Bible and on most occasions the "for ever" are a rendering of the word *'olam*. Where the translation is of a statute "for ever", *'olam* is used. Both words, *'ad 'olam* are used in Ex.12:24 regarding the passover. It was "an ordinance to thee and to thy sons *'ad 'olam*". The same applies to the twelve stones taken out of the Jordan River where the priests stood when the people crossed over. They were to be "for a memorial unto the children of Israel *'ad 'olam*". The passover sacrifice was taken away by Christ's one and final sacrifice and the stones no longer form a memorial nor can they be located. Hannah said to her husband that she will bring her son to appear before the Lord and "there abide for ever" (*'ad 'olam*). She later said to Eli that she "lent him to the Lord as long as he liveth" (1Sam. 1:22,28). Thus *'ad 'olam* meant in the case of Samuel until the end off his life and not until the end of time. David says in Psalm 21:4. "He asked life of thee and thou gavest him, even length of days of ever and ever, *'olam ve'ad'*, that is *'olam and 'ad'*, although he did not expect his days to last till the end of time. The Jews recognised that "for ever" does not necessarily mean until the end of the world, as can be seen in the case of Simon during the period of the Maccabees: "The Jews and the priests were well pleased that Simon should be their leader and high priest for ever, until there should arise a faithful prophet" (1Macc.14:41). "For ever" can therefore mean until an appointed time or a designated end. This, undoubtedly, is the true meaning of the words when applied to the promise of the land for ever and for an everlasting possession. The designated end was the coming of Christ in whom all the nations of the earth would be blessed. While the spiritual aspect of the covenant was eternal, its natural content regarding the land was temporal. Now, it is, "he that believeth on the Son hath everlasting life" and "my sheep hear my voice…and I give unto them eternal life" (Jn.3:36; 10:27,28). Canaan is no longer the consideration, but Heaven. God is the God of his people in the everlasting covenant with Abraham, which was not limited to his seed, but included all who believe, irrespective of their national origin (Ro.4:9–17). As far as the possession of the land was concerned, the time of its everlastingness was limited to the time of the incarnation of the Son of God.

Since the Lord Jesus Christ is the end of all the promises of spiritual blessings to mankind from the day on which Adam fell, it is reasonable to expect that the process which was ordained to ensure his coming was formulated to end with his coming. Once the end is accomplished, the instruments used for its accomplishment are no longer needed. This is the exact case with the election of Abraham and his seed in connection with the land of Canaan. The days of the Old Testament belonged to the Jewish people. The days subsequent to the New Testament belonged to the Gentiles. Jews have been saved in small numbers since. The trickle is becoming a stream and by God's grace will form a rushing mighty river. The biblical restoration of Israel is spiritual and not carnal. The political events of our day in the Middle East are in the will of God as everything else is in his will, including warfare and famine. But they do not form a part of the prophecies of the Bible regarding Israel.

About the Author

Salim Khalil Haddad was born in Palestine of Lebanese parents. He studied Medicine and Surgery in the universities of Cambridge and London and specialized in Neurosurgery in London. He is now retired and lives in Wales, United Kingdom.

www.ingramcontent.com/pod-product-compliance
Lightning Source LLC
Chambersburg PA
CBHW021128020426
42331CB00005B/677